ILLUSTRATED
KINGS AND QUEENS
OF ENGLAND

Dedications

To my friend Mónica.
Verity

To my father, Geoff, and in loving memory of my mother Margaret.
Tim

For my parents, Frank and Davida, with love.
Claire

Illustrated Kings and Queens of England

Copyright © 2016
MadeGlobal Publishing

ISBN-13: 978-84-945937-2-7

M
MadeGlobal Publishing

For more information on
MadeGlobal Publishing, visit our website:
www.madeglobal.com

Contents

Introduction 9
Ancient Britain 10
Alfred the Great 12
Edward the Elder 14
Aethelstan 16
Edmund I 18
Eadred 20
Eadwig 22
Edgar I 24
Edward the Martyr 26
Aethelred II 28
Sweyn Forkbeard 30
Edmund II 32
Cnut 34
Harold I 36
Harthacnut 38
Edward the Confessor 40
Harold II 42
William I, the Conqueror 44
William II 46
Henry I 48
Stephen 50
Henry II 52
Richard I 54
John 56
Henry III 58
Edward I 60
Edward II 62
Edward III 64
Richard II 66

Henry IV 68
Henry V 70
Henry VI 72
Edward IV 74
Edward V 76
Richard III 78
Henry VII 80
Henry VIII 82
Edward VI 84
Jane 86
Mary I 88
Elizabeth I 90
James I 92
Charles I 94
The Interregnum 96
Charles II 98
James II 100
William III & Mary II 102
Anne 104
George I 106
George II 108
George III 110
George IV 112
William IV 114
Victoria 116
Edward VII 118
George V 120
Edward VIII 122
George VI 124
Elizabeth II 126

Introduction

As a self-confessed royalist, it is my great pleasure to introduce you to the kings and queens who have all had a hand in making the United Kingdom what it is today. I could, of course, write a Bible-sized book about these monarchs, but I have chosen instead to give you a taster of their lives and reigns.

English history is full of characters who'd make ideal protagonists in block-buster novels - larger-than-life characters with soap opera style lives, swash-buckling warriors, saints, mad monarchs, virgin queens, religious zealots, regicides, alleged prince killers, Lotharios, romantic heroes, cake burners and tide-turners, monarchs with strange nicknames (Longshanks, the Unready, Ironside etc.), executed kings and tyrants - and that's just a few of them! It is hard to believe that some of them ever managed to lead a country or control governments and armies, while others had reigns that are known as "Golden Ages" for their advancements.

You will notice that the first monarch I introduce you to is Alfred the Great. He was not the first monarch of England, by any stretch of the imagination, but he was the first to claim to be "King of the English", or "King of the Anglo-Saxons".

When I found antique copies of John Cassell's volumes of "Illustrated History of England" I decided that his beautiful 19th century engravings should be shared for future generations to enjoy. Bringing these old images to life by adding colour became a bit of a family project and I was excited to get my daughter Verity involved – great for indoctrinating her with some history too! I believe that we have done justice to Cassell's original work.

I do hope you enjoy this journey through English history, I certainly enjoyed re-visiting the stories of these people.

Claire Ridgway

Lucar, Spain
November 2016

Ancient Britain

Britain was created in around 6100 BC, when a tsunami caused it to break free from continental Europe and become separated by what we know today as the English Channel. At that time, Britain was home to tribes of hunter-gatherers who had travelled there following food sources like reindeer and mammoth as they migrated.

Somewhere between 5000 and 4000 BC, farming was introduced to Britain, heralding the start of the New Stone Age or Neolithic Era. The Bronze Age began in around 2500 BC, when the "Beaker People" settled on the island and began making things from copper, gold and then bronze. In 750 BC, iron was introduced into Britain and started to replace bronze as the material used for tools and weapons. The people who worked with iron were the Celts, who were mainly farmers and who lived in groups and tribes ruled over by a king or queen.

The Romans were Britain's first invaders, crossing the English Channel in 43 AD and making Britain part of their empire. The Romans settled and lived in Britain until around 410 AD. They gave Britain its Roman roads, Roman baths, forts, the city of Londinium (London) and Hadrian's Wall. When the Romans left Britain, the Angles, Saxons and Jutes (known collectively as the Anglo-Saxons) invaded Britain by boat from Germany, Denmark and Holland. The Anglo-Saxons divided Britain into kingdoms but were never able to conquer Cornwall, Wales and Scotland. Notable Anglo-Saxon kings include Aethelbert of Kent (c.560-616), who was the first Anglo-Saxon king to embrace Christianity, which had been brought to Britain by St Augustine in 597 AD; Eadwin of Northumbria (c. 586-c. 633), who was the first Christian king in the north of England; and Offa, King of Mercia, who ruled from 757-796, and whose dominance of England spread all the way up to the Humber and east to the border with Wales, where he built Offa's Dyke.

In 793, the Vikings (or Norsemen) began their invasion of Britain from their homelands of Sweden, Denmark and Norway. Their first attacks were in Dorset and then on the monastery islands of Lindisfarne, just off the coast of Northumberland, and Iona, off the Scottish coast. In 829, Wessex became the most powerful kingdom in England, after King Egbert conquered Mercia and Northumbria, and in 843 the kingdom of Scotland was formed when the Pictish and Gaelic crowns merged. In 866, the Vikings launched attacks on northern England and East Anglia, and in 867 they captured York and made it their capital, naming it Jorvik. By 870 the Vikings had defeated the kings of Northumbria, East Anglia and Mercia, and so decided to attack Wessex, the only remaining Anglo-Saxon kingdom, ruled by King Aethelred. The Vikings defeated Aethelred's forces at the Battle of Reading, but Aethelred was victorious at the Battle of Ashdown. Unfortunately, this victory was followed by a series of defeats and Aethelred died on 23 April 871, leaving Wessex in the hands of his brother, Alfred.

Alfred the Great

849-899

Rule: 871-899

Marriages: Ealhswith

Issue: Aethelflaed Lady of the Mercians; Edward; Aethelgifu, Abbess of Shaftesbury; Aethelweard; Aelfthryth Countess of Flanders.

Alfred was born in Wantage, Oxfordshire, and was the fifth and youngest son of Aethelwulf, King of Wessex, and his first wife, Osburh. Alfred's brothers – Aethelstan, Aethelbald, Aethelbert and Aethelred – all ruled Wessex before him, with the crown passing from brother to brother, rather than to their sons. He inherited the throne of Wessex on Aethelred's death on 23 April 871 and was the first king to call himself King of the Anglo-Saxons, or English.

Although things looked bad at first for Alfred and Wessex, with the people of Wessex being forced to flee or surrender, and an attack on Chippenham forcing Alfred himself to withdraw into the Somerset marshes, Alfred was able to turn things around. He and his army defeated the Vikings at the Battle of Edington in May 878. Alfred then pursued the enemy to their stronghold in Chippenham, besieging their fortress. The siege ended after two weeks, when the starving Vikings surrendered and their leader, Guthrum, agreed to leave Wessex and convert to Christianity. Peace treaties between the two leaders saw England being divided up – the Vikings would rule northern and eastern England, and Alfred was to add West Mercia and Kent to his territories.

To protect his kingdom from any future threat, Alfred encouraged the building of burhs, or fortified towns, so that locals could man these defences in times of trouble. He was also responsible for creating a new and improved navy to fend off Viking invasions, and an army that worked on a "rota" basis. Alfred was also keen on reform, working hard to promote literacy by establishing schools and bringing law to his people.

Alfred died on 26 October 899 and was buried in the Old Minster, then moved to the New Minster, in Winchester. He was succeeded by his son Edward.

Trivia: According to legend, it was while Alfred was hiding in the Somerset marshes that he burned some cakes that a peasant woman had asked him to keep an eye on. The woman had no idea who he was and she gave him a good scolding.

Edward the Elder

c.874-924

Rule: 899-924

Marriages: Ecgwynn; Aelfflaed; Eadgifu of Kent

Issue: 14 children, including the future kings Aethelstan,
Edmund and Eadred, and St Edburga of Winchester.

Edward the Elder was the eldest son of Alfred the Great and Queen Ealhswith. Edward was able to build on the achievements of his father Alfred's reign and the military training he'd received. Not only was he able to defeat his cousin Aethelwold, who had his eye on the throne of Wessex and who joined forces with the Vikings at the Battle of the Holme, but he also defeated the Vikings at the Battle of Tettenhall in 909. A successful alliance with his sister Aethelflaed of Mercia, widow of King Aethelread of Mercia, against the Vikings helped him to extend the territories of Wessex and Mercia northwards. When Aetheflaed died in 918, leaving her young daughter as her successor, Edward was able to bring Mercia under his control.

Edward continued his father's work in building more burhs (or fortified towns) and was able to extend his kingdom, forcing the Vikings south of the Humber to submit to his authority. By the end of his reign, the Britons, Scots, Welsh and Vikings all acknowledged him as their "father and lord".

Edward died on 17 July 924 at Farndon-upon-Dee, a few days after quashing a Welsh/Mercian rebellion near Chester. His remains were taken to the New Minster in Winchester, the monastery that he himself had founded in 901, and buried there. He was succeeded by his son Aethelstan.

Trivia: Edward was not known as "Edward the Elder" in his lifetime. It was used in the 10th century by Wulfstan the Cantor in his *Vita S. Aethelwoldi* (Life of St Aethelwold) to distinguish him from Edward the Martyr.

Aethelstan

c.895-939

Rule: 924-939

Marriages: Did not marry

Issue: None

Aethelstan was the eldest son of Edward the Elder and his first wife Ecgwynn (or Egwina), and was brought up in Mercia by his aunt, Aethelflaed, who was married to Aethelred, Lord of the Mercians. Aethelflaed ruled Mercia after her husband died in 911 until her own death in 918, and Aethelstan became popular in the kingdom. Mercia proclaimed him king immediately after Edward's death, but the Council of Wessex deliberated and Aethelstan was not crowned until September 925.

In 927, Aethelstan invaded Northumbria and took York. The kingdoms of Scotland, Strathclyde and Bamburgh were also forced to submit to him, and the Welsh kings agreed to pay him a hefty annual tribute. In 937, the Scots and Vikings rebelled against him and invaded England, but Aethelstan, helped by his half-brother Edmund, was victorious at the Battle of Brunanburh.

Aethelstan is known for being an administrator and creating a centralised government. His kingdom was divided into shires run by ealdormen of his choosing who were also called to national assemblies. He was a lawmaker, introducing codes with harsh penalties for crimes like robbery. Aethelstan also issued a new coinage to regulate currency. It was known as the circumscription cross type and bore the inscription *Rex Totius Britanniae,* or King of the Whole of Britain.

He was a keen collector of art and religious relics, and gave much of his collection to monastic communities like that of St Cuthbert in Chester-le-Street.

Aethelstan died on 27 October 939 at Gloucester and was buried at Malmesbury Abbey. He was childless, and succeeded by Edmund.

Edmund I

921-946

Rule: 939-946

Marriages: Aelfgifu of Shaftesbury; Aethelflaed of Damerham.

Issue: Eadwig, King of England; Edgar, King of England.

Edmund was the son of Edward the Elder and his third wife Eadgifu of Kent, and the half-brother of Aethelstan. He was only eighteen years old when his half-brother died in 939, but had helped Aethelstan defeat the Scots and Vikings in the Battle of Brunanburh when he was just sixteen. He was crowned king on 16 November 939.

He immediately faced trouble from Olaf Guthfrithsson, who took Northumbria and then invaded the Midlands. Edmund lost much of Northumbria to Olaf but was able to reconquer the Midlands after Olaf's death in 942 and by 945 had reconquered Northumbria and conquered Strathclyde, which he then gave to his ally, King Malcom I of Scotland.

Just before he died, Edmund sent envoys to France to Duke Hugh the Great, who was holding King Louis IV of France hostage. Edmund hoped to negotiate the restoration of Louis, who had spent time in England in exile, but Edmund died before negotiations could be completed.

Edmund was murdered by a robber named Leofa, who stabbed him in the stomach on 26 May 946 at Pucklechurch, Gloucestershire. He was buried at Glastonbury Abbey. He was succeeded by his brother Eadred.

EDMUND I.

Eadred

c.923-955

Rule: 946-955

Marriages: Did not marry.

Issue: None

Eadred (or Edred) was the second son of Edward the Elder and his third wife Eadgifu of Kent. He became king in May 946, after the murder of his brother Edmund I, and was crowned at Kingston-upon-Thames by Archbishop Oda of Canterbury on 16 August 946.

Like his brother Edmund, Eadred had to deal with trouble in the North - Olaf Sihtricson (or Amlaíb Cuarán), former King of Northumbria, who managed to regain York. Olaf was, however, driven out by the Northumbrians who first submitted to Eadred and then changed their allegiance to Eric Bloodaxe, former King of Norway. Although Eadred and his forces were defeated by Eric at the Battle of Castleford, the Northumbrians were frightened that Eadred would make them suffer for their defiance and so submitted to him, recognising him as their king and expelling Eric from York. Eric was killed in 954 by Osulf, Lord of Bamborough and an ally of Eadred.

One of Eadred's chief advisers was St Dunstan, who refused to take the offices of bishop of Winchester and bishop of Crediton because of his commitment to the king.

Eadred is known to have suffered from some kind of digestive disorder, which caused him to have problems swallowing solid food. He died on 23 November 955 at Frome in Somerset and was buried in the Old Minster at Winchester. His bones are now in Winchester Cathedral in a mortuary chest which can still be seen today.

Eadred died childless, so was succeeded by his nephew Eadwig.

EDRED.

Eadwig

c.939-959

Rule: 955-959

Marriages: Aelfgifu (annulled).

Issue: None

Eadwig, also known as Edwy the Fair or Edwig All-Fair, was the son of Edmund I and his first wife Aelfgifu of Shaftesbury. He became king at the age of sixteen (some say thirteen) on the death of his uncle and was crowned at Kingston-upon-Thames in January 956. According to legend, he missed his coronation feast and was found in bed with a noblewoman named Aelfgifu - some say that her mother Aethelgith was also in bed with them. Eadwig was dragged back to the proceedings by Dunstan, Bishop of London, and although the couple later married, their marriage was forcibly annulled in 958 by Archbishop Oda on the grounds of consanguinity (relationship by blood). Dunstan later fled to Flanders after falling out with Eadwig, Eadwig having never forgiven him for his actions on his coronation day.

During Eadwig's short reign, his kingdom was divided, with Mercia and Northumbria becoming controlled by his brother Edgar, while Eadwig kept control of Wessex and Kent. Sources do not agree as to whether this was the result of rebellion or Eadwig ceding control to his brother.

Eadwig is known for the large amount of charters issued in his reign. Over sixty were issued in 956 and, although these gifts of land can be seen as generous, they were probably more to do with buying people's loyalty.

Eadwig died on 1 October 959 and was succeeded by Edgar. It is not known what he died of and some deem it to have been a suspicious death.

Edgar I

943-975

Rule: 959-975

Marriages: Aethelflaed; Aelfthryth

Issue: Edward, King of England; Saint Edith of Wilton; Edmund of England; Aethelred, King of England.

Edgar I, also known as Edgar the Peacemaker (or Peaceful), was the second son of Edmund I and his wife Aelfgifu of Shaftesbury. He was only young when his parents died and so was brought up by Aethelstan Half-King, the Ealdorman of East Anglia, and his wife, Aelfwynn. Edgar inherited the throne on the death of his brother Eadwig in 959, but was not crowned until 973, when he and his wife Aelfthryth were crowned together on 11 May at Bath. Aelfthryth was the first queen consort to be officially crowned as queen of England.

At the age of sixteen, he married Aethelflaed but went on to have an affair with a nun named Wulthryth, which resulted in the birth of St Edith of Wilton. Aethelflaed died in 963 and Edgar went on to marry Aelfthryth, daughter of Ordgar, ealdorman of Devon, and widow of Aethelwald, ealdorman of East Anglia.

His reign is known for being a peaceful one. He was already ruling Mercia and Northumbria when he inherited his brother's crown and became King of Wessex. He united his kingdoms with new uniform coinage and new laws. Unlike his brother, he got on with Bishop Dunstan and so brought him back from his exile and made him Archbishop of Canterbury. Dunstan acted as Edgar's chief adviser and it is likely that their close friendship was responsible for Edgar becoming a patron of monastic reform and Benedictine reformers.

Edgar is also known for his law-making, his reform of coinage in 973 and the peace of his reign, which appears to have been more down to his control through military force rather than his "peaceful" nature.

Edgar died on 8 July 975 at Winchester and was buried at Glastonbury Abbey. He was succeeded by his son Edward.

Edward the Martyr

c.962-978

Rule: 975-978

Marriages: Did not marry.

Issue: None

Edward the Martyr was the eldest son of Edgar I by his first wife Aethelflaed. He was only thirteen when he became king in 975, and he was crowned at Kingston-upon-Thames, probably in that same year.

The sudden death of his father and his young age led to trouble, with the succession being disputed. Archbishop Dunstan and Aethelwine, ealdorman of East Anglia, supported Edward's claim to the throne, while the Bishop of Winchester and Aelfhere, ealdorman of Mercia, supported that of Aethelred, Edward's younger half-brother. Edward was murdered on 18 March 878 at Corfe, while on his way to visit Aethelred at Corfe Castle. His body was buried secretly at Wareham and then buried properly at Shaftesbury Abbey after his remains were recovered in 979.

There are four theories regarding Edward's murder:

- That he was murdered by supporters of Aethelred

- That his murder was plotted by Aethelred

- That Aelfhere, ealdorman of Mercia, was responsible

- That his stepmother, Aelfthryth, plotted his death.

Although he is known as Edward the Martyr, Edward was never canonised by the Catholic Church.

Aethelred II

c.968-1016

Rule: 978-1013, 1014-1016

Marriages: Aelfgifu of York; Emma of Normandy

Issue: 6 sons (Aethelstan; Ecgberht; Edmund Ironside; Eadred; Eadwig; Edgar) and
4 or 5 daughters by Aelfgifu;
2 sons (Edward the Confessor; Alfred) and
1 daughter (Godu, Countess of Boulogne) by Emma.

Aethelred II, or Aethelred the Unready as he's more commonly known, inherited the throne after the murder of his half-brother in 978. He was crowned at Kingston-upon-Thames on 14 April 979 by Archbishop Dunstan. He was only around ten years of age (some say just seven) when he became king and so relied on the advice of those around him. It is thought that his nickname, "the Unready", comes from the Old English "unraed", or "bad counsel", and refers to the poor advice he received from those wanting to take advantage of the boy king after the deaths of the Bishop of Winchester and ealdorman of Mercia, his former advisers.

The peace that England had experienced under Edgar and Edward was shattered in 980 when the Vikings began a series of raids, attacking the coasts of Kent, Hampshire, Dorset, Devon and Cornwall. In 1002, Aethelred married Emma of Normandy, daughter of Duke Richard II of Normandy, hoping that Richard would swap his allegiance from the Vikings to Aethelred. He didn't. Aethelred decided to punish the Vikings, ordering the massacre of all Danes in England on St Brice's Day, 13 November 1002. It was an impossible feat, and only stirred up more trouble with Sweyn Forkbeard, King of Denmark, who sacked Norwich in 1004 out of revenge, and led several campaigns in the south and the Midlands over the next few years.

In 1013, Sweyn decided to invade with the aim of replacing Aethelred as king. Aethelred was forced to flee to the Isle of Wight and then Normandy, and Sweyn was accepted as king. After Sweyn's death, Aethelred came back and ruled until his own death on 23 April 1016, leaving his son Edmund to inherit the throne.

ETHELRED II.

Sweyn Forkbeard

d. 1014

Rule: King of Denmark 986-1014,
King of Norway 986-995 and 999-1014,
King of England 1013-1014.

Marriages: Gunhilda of Poland, Sigrid the Haughty

Issue: 8 children including Harald II of Denmark and King Cnut.

Sweyn Forkbeard was the son of Harald Bluetooth, King of Denmark and Norway. His reign in England was a short one. He had been declared King of England on Christmas Day 1013, after he had invaded England and King Aethelred had fled into exile, but he died in Gainsborough, Lincolnshire, just a few weeks later, on 3 February 1014. His remains were taken back to Denmark where his eldest son Harald succeeded him. Although the Vikings proclaimed Sweyn's son Cnut as King of England, the royal council in England sent for Aethelred, who defeated Cnut's army and drove Cnut out of England.

Sweyn had coins made with his likeness in the center. nscription on the coins is in Latin and reads "ZVEN REX DÆNOR[UM]", which translates as reading "Sven, King of the Danes".

Trivia: The royal house in Denmark today descends from Sweyn through his daughter Estrid Svendsdatterd. James I of England also descended from Sweyn through his great-grandfather James IV of Scotland, whose mother was Margaret of Denmark.

Edmund II

c.989-1016

Rule: 23 April 1016 – 30 November 1016

Marriages: Ealdgyth, widow of Sigeferth, chief thegn of the Seven Burghs.

Issue: Edward the Exile; Edmund Aetheling

Edmund II, also known as Edmund Ironside or Eadmund II, was the third son of Aethelred the Unready and his first wife Aelfgifu of York. He was crowned king in St Paul's Cathedral, London, in May 1016, and spent the seven months of his reign battling against Sweyn Forkbeard's son Cnut. Cnut was victorious and this led to a peace treaty in which Edmund ceded Northumbria and Mercia to Cnut, while he kept Wessex.

Edmund died on 30 November 1016 and was buried at Glastonbury Abbey. Cnut became King of England and sent Edmund's sons to Sweden, where they were subsequently sent to Kiev and then on to Hungary.

EDMUND IRONSIDE

Cnut

c.995-1035

Rule: King of England 1016-1035, King of Denmark 1018-1035, King of Norway 1028-1035.

Marriages: Aelfgifu of Northampton; Emma of Normandy.

Issue: Sweyn Knutsson, King of Norway; Harold Harefoot, King of England, by Aelfgifu; Harthacnut, King of Denmark & England; Gunhilda, Holy Roman Empress, by Emma.

Cnut (also known as Canute and Knut Sveinsson) was the second son of Sweyn Forkbeard and his first wife, Gunhilda of Poland. When the royal council in England refused to acknowledge Cnut as his father's successor in 1014, he returned to Denmark and gathered his forces. In 1015, he landed at Poole, on the south coast of England, and began his fight for England against Aethelred. By Aethelred's death in April 1016, Cnut had captured large parts of the country and his claim to the throne was supported by not only the nobility, but also the church. However, Aethelred's son, Edmund, was crowned King Edmund II in London.

After months of battles over the summer of 1016, Cnut defeated Edmund at the Battle of Assandun (Ashingdon) in Essex. The country was divided between Edmund and Cnut, and, when Edmund died just a few weeks later, Cnut claimed the throne of England and was crowned in St Paul's Cathedral in January 1017.

In July 1017, Cnut married Aethelred's widow, Emma of Normandy, putting aside his first wife Aelfgifu of Northampton, who was never recognised as his legal wife and queen. In 1018, his brother Harald II of Denmark died and Cnut succeeded to the Danish throne. While he was away in Denmark, he left England's four earldoms in the hands of Danish earls, and then later English noblemen who had shown themselves to be trustworthy.

Cnut's reign was successful and he has gone down in history as a strong, effective leader and a patron of the church. He died at Shaftesbury, Dorset, on 12 November 1035 and was buried at Winchester Cathedral. He was succeeded in England by his son Harold Harefoot (Harold I) and in Denmark by his son Harthacnut.

Trivia: According to the twelfth century historian Henry of Huntingdon, King Cnut rebuked his flattering courtiers and showed his humility by sitting on his throne near the sea and commanding the incoming tide to stop. The tide continued to come in, soaking the king's feet and legs, and Cnut declared "Let all men know how empty and worthless is the power of kings, for there is none worthy of the name, but He whom heaven, earth, and sea obey by eternal laws."

Harold I

c.1015-1040

Rule: 1035-1040

Marriages: Did not marry.

Issue: Aelfwine, an illegitimate son who became a monk in a monastery in Aquitaine, France.

On King Cnut's death in 1035, Cnut's eldest son Harold, also known as Harold Harefoot, was not recognised as king because his mother, Aelfgifu of Northampton, had never been recognised as Cnut's legal wife. The crown passed to Harthacnut, Cnut's eldest son by Emma of Normandy, who had also become King of Denmark, although Harold was given control of Mercia and Northumbria while Emma acted as regent for Harthacnut in Wessex.

Threats to Denmark from Norway kept Harthacnut away from England. In 1037 Harold was made king of the whole of England and Emma fled into exile in Flanders. His success at claiming the crown appears to be down to the support of Godwine, Earl of Wessex, who had previously sided with Harthacnut.

Harold died on 17 March 1040 at Oxford at the age of just twenty-four, saving Harthacnut the trouble of invading and fighting for the crown. He was initially buried at Westminster Abbey but his resting place was desecrated and his remains exhumed and beheaded, before being thrown into a fen. His body was re-interred in the church of St Clement Danes, in the City of Westminster, London, after it was recovered from the fen by local fishermen.

Trivia: According to the 12th century monk Florence, or Florentius, of Worcester, Queen Aelfgifu actually adopted Harold and he was really the son of a cobbler. This is now thought to be a tale spread by Emma of Normandy to discredit Harold. His nickname "Harefoot" is thought to refer to his speed and skill as a hunter.

Harthacnut

c.1018-1042

Rule: King of Denmark 1035-1042, King of England 1040-1042.

Marriages: Did not marry

Issue: None

Harthacnut, also known as Hardicanute (Hardecanute/Hardeknud) and Cnut (Canute) III, was the son of King Cnut by his second wife Emma of Normandy. He had become King of Denmark, as Cnut III, on his father's death in 1035, and King of England on 17 March 1040. He had been in the midst of organising an attack on England to claim the throne when his half-brother Harold died. He landed at Sandwich in Kent in June 1040, with his mother Emma, and was crowned king at Canterbury Cathedral on 18 June.

Harthacnut held his half-brother responsible for the murder of Alfred the Aetheling (one of Emma of Normandy's sons by Aethelred the Unready) and so desecrated Harold's tomb at Westminster Abbey.

Harthacnut was only King of England for two years. On 8 June 1042, he died after consuming copious amounts of alcohol at a wedding banquet. He had suffered previous bouts of ill-health (some historians believe that he suffered from tuberculosis) and it is thought that his death was caused by a stroke or heart-attack. The 13th century Old Norse saga, the *Morkinskinna*, puts Harthacnut's death down to poison. According to the saga, Aelfgifu of Northampton was trying to poison Magnus I of Norway, who was visiting Harthacnut's court, but Harthacnut drank from the horn instead. Harthacnut was buried at the Old Minster in Winchester. He was succeeded by his half-brother Edward.

Trivia: Hardeknud means "tough knot" in Danish.

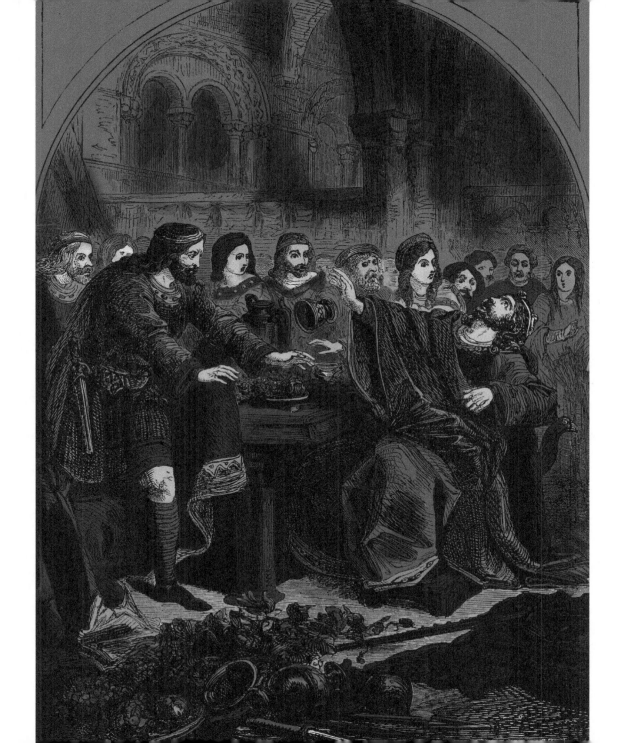

Edward the Confessor

c.1005-1066

Rule:	1042-1066
Marriages:	Eadgyth (Edith), daughter of Earl Godwine of Wessex.
Issue:	None

Edward was the eldest son of Aethelred II (the Unready) by his second wife Emma of Normandy, and he was the great-great-great-grandson of Alfred the Great. He had been sent into exile in Normandy with his brother Alfred when Cnut became king. Alfred was murdered when the brothers returned to England in 1036, when Harold Harefoot and Harthacnut were arguing over the throne, but Edward managed to flee back to Normandy. He became King of England on the death of his half-brother Harthacnut in 1042, after being recognised as his heir when he came to England in 1041, and was crowned at Winchester Cathedral on Easter Sunday 1043.

In 1045, Edward married Eadgyth, daughter of Godwine of Wessex, one of the most powerful men in England. But Edward's links to Normandy and the influence of his Norman favourites caused problems and in 1051 things came to a head when Edward chose Robert of Jumièges (Robert Champart), a Norman, as Archbishop of Canterbury instead of a man related to Godwine. Godwine rebelled but he and his family were forced into exile and Edward put aside Eadgyth, sending her to a nunnery. In 1052, Godwine returned to England with an army and was able to secure significant support in England. To avoid civil war, Edward restored Godwine to his title, took Eadgyth back as his queen and dismissed his Norman archbishop.

Edward is known for the construction of Westminster Abbey, which was begun in c.1050 on the site of an old monastery. The majority of English monarchs, from William the Conqueror onwards, have been crowned in the Abbey. The Abbey was consecrated on 28 December 1065.

As the childless Edward lay in a coma in 1065, there were four possible claimants to his throne: Edgar the Aetheling (grandson of Edmund II); William of Normandy, who claimed that Edward had chosen him as his successor; Harold, son of Godwine of Wessex, who also claimed Edward had chosen him; and Harold Hardrada,King of Norway, whose claim went back to the agreement between King Harthacnut and his father that if either of them died without issue the other would inherit their kingdom.

Edward died on the 4 or 5 January 1066 and was buried on 6 January at Westminster Abbey. Miracles became associated with him and in 1102 his body was examined and found not to have decayed. He was canonised in 1161 by Pope Alexander III and reburied in 1269 in a specially built shrine in Westminster Abbey.

Harold II

c.1022-1066

Rule: 4/5 January 1066 – 14 October 1066

Marriages: Eadgyth (Edith Swannesha); Ealdgyth of Mercia

Issue: 6 children with Eadgyth; 2 sons, Harold and Ulf, with Ealdgyth.

Harold II was the last of the Anglo-Saxon kings and became king in January 1066 on the death of his brother-in-law, Edward the Confessor. Harold was the son of Godwine, Earl of Essex, one of the most powerful men in England, and came to the throne after proving his loyalty to the king by undertaking expeditions and diplomatic missions, and was chosen as Edward's successor by the royal council. He was crowned on 7 January 1066 at Westminster Abbey.

Harold had made an enemy of his brother Tostig, Earl of Northumbria, in late 1065 when Harold had supporting Northumbrian rebels revolting against Tostig's taxes and Tostig had been dismissed as Earl of Northumbria. Tostig allied himself with Harald Hardrada of Norway and the two men launched an attack on England in September 1066, landing near Scarborough and laying siege to York. Harold defeated them at the Battle of Stamford Bridge and both Harald and Tostig were killed in the fighting. Unfortunately, Harold then received news that William, Duke of Normandy, and his forces had landed on the coast of East Sussex. Harold quickly marched his army down from Yorkshire, recruiting new men on the way, and the two armies met at Senlac Hill, near Hastings, on 14 October 1066, in a battle known as the Battle of Hastings. Harold was killed, along with his brothers Gyrth and Leofwine, and his forces were defeated. An image on the Bayeux Tapestry has led to the story that Harold was killed by an arrow in the eye, but it is not known whether that man is actually Harold. William the Conqueror built Battle Abbey on the battle site, the high altar of the church marking the spot where Harold was killed.

It is thought that Harold was buried at Waltham Abbey.

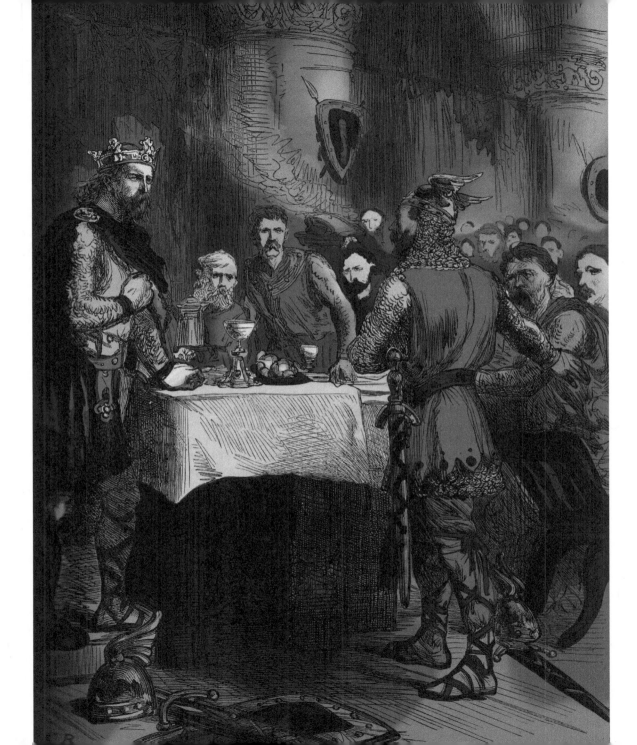

William I, the Conqueror

c.1028-1087

Rule: 1066-1087

Marriages: Matilda of Flanders.

Issue: At least 9 children, inc. Robert Curthose; William Rufus; Henry; Adela of Blois.

William I, also known as William the Conqueror and William the Bastard, was the illegitimate son of Robert I, Duke of Normandy (also known as Robert the Magnificent and Robert the Devil) and his mistress Herleva, and on his father's death in 1035 he was accepted as Duke of Normandy. William married Matilda, daughter of Count Baldwin V of Flanders, in the 1050s.

When Harold became King of England in January 1066, William, who claimed that Edward the Confessor had named him as his heir, set about organising an invasion. William was even able to obtain the pope's blessing for his invasion, and on 28 September 1066 he and his forces landed at Pevensey in East Sussex. He defeated Harold at the Battle of Hastings on 14 October 1066, but Edgar the Aetheling was declared king and it took further military campaigning in Hampshire and Berkshire for the royal council to submit and accept William as king. He was crowned on Christmas Day 1066 at Westminster Abbey.

In 1067 and 1068, William was able to quash a rebellion in the south-west of England and the Welsh Marches, but there was more trouble to come. In 1069, Edgar the Aetheling attacked York and then Sweyn of Denmark joined forces with Edgar, attacking the Yorkshire coast and York. This caused an uprising in Northumbria and William reacted ruthlessly with his "Harrying of the North", which saw him burning York, killing livestock, killing people and leaving survivors to succumb to starvation. It is thought that up to 150,000 people died. There was further trouble, with uprisings in East Anglia and the North, but they were defeated in 1075.

William is known for his castles which were of a motte and bailey design and built first of wood and then upgraded to stone. Norman barons held them on behalf of the king. More than eighty castles were built during his reign. He also changed the language at court because French was the dominant language of the king, the court and the elite. The French words we have in our modern English language date back to this time.

William is also known for The Domesday Book. This first national census, which was commissioned in 1085, was a survey of England and Wales for tax and administration purposes. It was a full record of each landholder and their holdings.

William died on 9 September 1087 at the Priory of St Gervais, near Rouen, following a fall from his horse while riding into battle at Mantes. While dying, he entrusted the care of Normandy to his eldest son Robert, and England to his second son William Rufus. William is buried at the Abbey of Saint-Étienne, Caen.

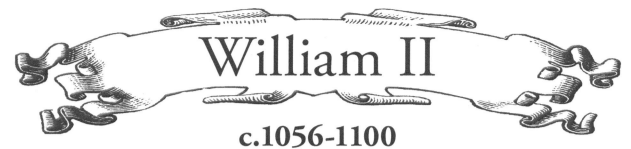

William II

c.1056-1100

Rule: 1087-1100

Marriages: Did not marry.

Issue: None

William II, also known as William Rufus due to his ruddy complexion, was the third son of William the Conqueror and Matilda of Flanders. After being chosen by his dying father as his successor in England, William travelled there and was crowned by Archbishop Lanfranc on 26 September 1087 at Westminster Abbey.

Nobles who held land in both Normandy and England were concerned about having different rulers in Normandy and England, and so rebelled against William in England in 1088 with the aim of replacing him with his older brother Robert, who had inherited Normandy from his father. William successfully quashed the rebellion and went on to invade Normandy. The brothers came to an understanding and when Robert went crusading in 1096, William ruled Normandy and controlled it until his death in 1100.

William enjoyed good relations with the church in the first two years of his reign, but after Archbishop Lanfranc's death in 1089 William delayed appointing a replacement and began appropriating ecclesiastical revenue for himself. In 1093, when he was seriously ill, William appointed Anselm, Abbot of Bec, as his Archbishop of Canterbury, but Anselm was keen on reform and spoke out against William using church funds. This led to a breakdown in their relationship and Anselm was forced into exile, leaving William to continue using the church as his personal kitty.

William was killed on 2 August 1100 when he was accidentally "shot by an arrow by one of his own men" (*Anglo-Saxon Chronicle*) while hunting in the New Forest. The "Rufus Stone" marks the spot where he is thought to have fallen. He was buried at Winchester Cathedral.

Henry I

c.1068-1135

Rule: 1100-1135

Marriages: Matilda (born Edith) of Scotland; Adeliza of Louvain

Issue: Matilda and William Adelin by Matilda. Also a number of illegitimate children.

Henry I, also known as Henry "Beauclerc" (fine scholar) , was the youngest son of William I and succeeded to the English throne on the death of his brother William II, after his claim to the throne was supported by barons led by Henry de Beaumont and Robert of Meulan. On hearing the news of his brother's death, Henry seized the royal treasury at Winchester Castle and was then proclaimed king, being crowned on 5 August at Westminster Abbey by Maurice, Bishop of London. He issued a coronation charter promising to govern the country well, to fight the abuses and injustice of his brother's reign, to return to the laws of Edward the Confessor and to establish peace. He recalled Archbishop Anselm from exile and threw unpopular members of his brother's government, including Ranulf Flambard Bishop of Durham, into the Tower of London for corruption.

In November 1100, Henry married Edith, daughter of Malcom III of Scotland, thus forming a bond between England and Scotland. Edith then changed her name to Matilda, a Norman name.

In 1101, Flambard escaped from the Tower of London and fled to Normandy, where he joined with Henry's brother Robert and began organising an invasion of England. The invasion never happened and the brothers made peace by treaty in August 1101, with Robert renouncing his claim to the English throne. However, Henry invaded Normandy in 1105 and 1106, and defeated Robert in the Battle of Tinchebrai, capturing Robert and keeping him prisoner until Robert's death in 1134.

Henry lost his two legitimate sons in 1120 when the White Ship sank in the English Channel. His surviving legitimate child was a daughter, Matilda, who Henry named as his successor after his second wife, Adeliza, bore him no children. Matilda was the widow of Henry V, Holy Roman Emperor.

Henry died on 1 December 1135 at Lyons-la-Forêt after eating a dish of lampreys (fish). He was buried at Reading Abbey, although his brain and some of his other organs were buried at Rouen.

Henry was an effective ruler, albeit rather harsh at times, who is known for centralising the administration of his two kingdoms and using advisers in England and viceroys in Normandy to look after his kingdoms while he was away. He established peace in England, through his alliance with Scotland, and his reign saw the development of the royal exchequer, a reformation of coinage and an expansion of the justice system.

Stephen

c.1096-1154

Rule: 1135-1141

Marriages: Matilda of Boulogne, daughter of Eustace III, Count of Boulogne.

Issue: Baldwin of Blois; Eustace IV; William; Marie. He also had 3 illegitimate children.

Stephen was the son of Stephen Count of Blois and his wife Adela, daughter of William I. He was also the nephew of Henry I. Although Henry I had named his daughter Empress Matilda as his successor, Stephen was nearer to England, being in Boulogne at the time of Henry's death, and so seized power while Matilda was in Anjou with her second husband, Geoffrey of Anjou. Stephen was crowned at Westminster Abbey on 22 December 1135. His kingship was supported by Roger, Bishop of Salibury and Henry I's Lord Chancellor, Henry of Blois (Stephen's younger brother and the Bishop of Winchester), and Robert of Gloucester, Henry I's illegitimate son.

Just after Stephen's coronation, David I of Scotland, who supported Empress Matilda's claim to the throne, marched on England. The two kings came to an agreement, but David invaded again in 1136, 1137 and 1138. After a series of skirmishes a settlement was again agreed upon, with David keeping Carlisle and Cumberland and Stephen retaining Bamburgh and Newcastle.

In 1138, Robert of Gloucester rebelled against Stephen and swapped sides to that of his half-sister Matilda, and on 30 September 1139 Matilda, Robert and an army landed at Arundel with the aim of Matilda claiming the throne. Thus began years of civil war. Stephen was captured at Lincoln in February 1141 and Matilda declared herself queen, but Stephen was released in November 1141 when Robert of Gloucester was captured and an exchange of hostages was agreed upon. Matilda retired to Normandy in 1147 after the death of Robert, but her eldest son Henry kept up the pressure on Stephen and led expeditions to England in 1149 and 1153. Stephen's son and heir, Eustace, died in August 1153 and in November 1153 the Treaty of Winchester was agreed between Stephen and Henry, and Stephen recognised Henry as his successor. Stephen died on 25 October 1154 at a priory in Dover and was buried at Faversham Abbey.

Henry II

1133-1189

Rule: 1154-1189

Marriages: Eleanor of Aquitaine.

Issue: William; Henry "the Young King"; Richard I; Geoffrey, Duke of Brittany; Matilda, Duchess of Saxony; Eleanor of England, Queen of Castile; Joan, Queen of Sicily; John, King of England.
He also had several illegitimate children, including Geoffrey, Archbishop of York; William de Longespee, Earl of Salisbury.

Henry II, also known as Henry Curtmantle (due to his short cloaks) and Henry Fitzempress, was the son of Empress Matilda and her second husband Geoffrey of Anjou. He inherited Normandy from his mother and Anjou from his father, and his marriage to Eleanor of Aquitaine in 1152 gave him further territory in France. In 1154, he inherited the throne of England on the death of King Stephen and was crowned with Eleanor on 19 December 1154. His vast empire stretched all the way from the Pyrenees in France right up to the English border with Scotland. Twenty-one years of his reign were spent away from England, dealing with his territories in France, but his use of viceroys kept trouble at bay in England.

Henry is known for his legal reforms: trial by jury, rather than trial by ordeal, became the norm during his reign; and the Treatise of Glanvill, the first legal textbook, was produced.

In 1170, Thomas Becket, Henry's Archbishop of Canterbury and chief adviser, was murdered following a disagreement between the two men over church-state relations. According to tradition, Henry cried out in a rage, "Who will rid me of this turbulent priest?" and four of his knights cut Becket down on 29 December 1170 in Canterbury Cathedral. Becket was promptly recognised as a martyr by the church and canonised by Pope Alexander III in February 1173.

Henry's later years are known for the squabbling between his sons, Richard, John and Geoffrey, and their revolt against him. In 1183, Richard joined forces with his father in a campaign in Aquitaine and Henry decided to appoint Richard as his successor in England, with his lands in Aquitaine going to John. This decision caused even more trouble between the brothers and their father, and Henry died on 6 July 1189 at Chinon Castle, in Anjou, while he was at war with Richard, who had joined forces with Philip Augustus, King of France. Henry was buried first at Fontevraud Abbey and then in Westminster Abbey.

Richard I

1157-1199

Rule: 1189-1199

Marriages: Berengaria of Navarre.

Issue: Philip of Cognac (illegitimate).

Richard I, also known as Richard the Lionheart (Coeur de Lion) or Richard the Crusader, was the third son of Henry II and Eleanor of Aquitaine. His older brothers, William and Henry, both died before their father and so Richard inherited the English throne on the death of his father in 1189. He was invested as Duke of Normandy in July 1189 and crowned King of England on 3 September 1189 at Westminster Abbey.

On 12 December 1189, Richard left England to go on crusade. He was victorious at Acre, Arsuf and Jaffa and was on his way home back to England in December 1192 when he was captured by Leopald V, Duke of Austria, near Vienna, and then handed to Henry VI, Holy Roman Emperor. Richard's brother John took advantage of Richard's four-year absence by declaring that Richard was dead and by plotting to take the throne. He seized Windsor Castle and planned uprisings and an invasion of England by Flemish mercenaries. However, the brothers' mother, Eleanor of Aquitaine, was able to put John in his place and to obtain Richard's release by raising the required ransom. On his return to England, Richard forgave John and named him his heir. Richard was re-crowned king in 1194 at Winchester.

Richard died on 6 April 1199 from gangrene in a wound sustained from a crossbow bolt to the shoulder, while laying siege to the castle of Châlus, the home of Viscount Aimar V of Limoges, who had risen up in rebellion. Richard's heart was buried at Rouen, while his entrails were buried in Châlus and his body at Fontrevaud Abbey.

Trivia: His nickname "the Lionheart" stems from his reputation as a great warrior. He was also known as "Ricart Oc-e-No" ("Richard Yes and No" in Occitan) in southwest France, allegedly due to his curtness. Some historians are challenging his reputation as a great king and hero, pointing out how he never learned English, didn't like England and only used the kingdom to raise money.

John

1167-1216

Rule:	1199-1216
Marriages:	Isabella, Countess of Gloucester (dissolved after his accession); Isabella, Countess of Angoulême.
Issue:	With his second wife: Henry III; Richard 1st Earl of Cornwall; Joan Queen of Scotland; Isabella Holy Roman Empress; Eleanor Countess of Pembroke.

John, also known as John Lackland, due to the fact that as fourth child his father did not promise him any territory, was born on 24 December 1167 at Beaumont Palace, Oxford. He was the youngest son of Henry II of England and Eleanor of Aquitaine. He was crowned on 27 May 1199 at Westminster Abbey. His brother Richard I had named him as his heir, but there was another claimant, Arthur of Brittany, son of Geoffrey, John's elder brother, who had the support of a number of French barons and also Philip II of France. However, in 1200 John and Philip signed the Treaty of Le Goulet, in which Philip recognised John as heir of Richard and as King of England, and John acknowledged Philip as his overlord in France. Arthur went on to challenge John in 1202, by campaigning in Normandy, but was taken captive at Mirebeau and imprisoned. Arthur then disappeared and this has led to the idea that he was murdered on the orders of John. His death is still a mystery.

By 1204, John had lost Normandy and Anjou to Philip II and his only French territory was the Duchy of Aquitaine. His desire to recapture his former territories led to him levying taxes in England to finance his campaigns, which, in turn, made him an unpopular king. He also quarrelled with the pope and was excommunicated for a time.

Civil war broke out in England in 1215, due to the barons' many grievances, and this led to John signing the Magna Carta, or The Great Charter of the Liberties of England, at Runnymede on the banks of the Thames in June 1215. This charter limited the monarch's powers, confirmed the liberties of the church and laid out the feudal obligations of the barons. It also set up a council of barons whose job it was to ensure that the monarch complied with the charter. It is seen as the first written constitution in the history of Europe. John only signed the charter as a stalling tactic and got the Pope to annul it.

John died on 18 or 19 October at Newark Castle after becoming ill following a meal of peaches and ale. He was buried at Worcester Cathedral.

Henry III

1207-1272

Rule: 1216-1272

Marriages: Eleanor of Provence.

Issue: Edward I; Margaret, Queen of Scots; Beatrice, Countess of Richmond; Edmund Crouchback, 1st Earl of Leicester and Lancaster; Katherine.

Henry was born on 1 October 1207 at Winchester Castle and was the son of King John and Isabella of Angoulême. He inherited the throne at the age of nine and is one of England's longest reigning monarchs. He was crowned on 28 October 1207 at Gloucester Abbey and inherited a kingdom troubled by civil war (the First Barons' War). His father had appointed a council and had chosen William Marshal, 1st Earl of Pembroke, to help Henry in his minority. When Marshal died in 1219, Hugh de Burgh took over as regent until Henry assumed control in January 1227.

Henry's priority was the restoration of the French territories lost in his father's reign. However, his French campaigns were costly failures and these, combined with his plans to extort money from the clergy in order to pay the pope for his acquisition of Sicily, led to further trouble with the barons of England. The barons, led by Simon de Monfort, 6th Earl of Leicester, revolted in 1258, insisting on reform, and this led to Parliament passing the Provisions of Oxford, which created a council of fifteen elected by the barons to rule alongside the king. This constitution was replaced in 1259 by the Provisions of Westminster. Henry repudiated the Provisions by papal bull in 1261 and so civil war broke out again in 1264. Henry, his queen and his son Edward were taken prisoner by Simon de Montfort and the rebel barons, and de Montfort took control of government.

In May 1265, Henry's son Edward escaped and joined forces with the Earl of Gloucester. In August, the two men met de Montfort and his army at the Battle of Evesham. De Montfort was killed and his forces defeated. Henry was released and restored as king, but Edward, as Steward of England, took more control.

Henry died on 16 November 1272 at Westminster and was buried at Westminster Abbey.

Edward I

1239-1307

Rule: 1272-1307

Marriages: Eleanor of Castile; Marguerite of France

Issue: 14 children (some say 16) from his first marriage, including
Eleanor, Countess of Bar; Joan of Acre, Countess of Hertford; Alphonso, Earl of
Chester; Margaret, Duchess of Brabant; Mary of Woodstock; Elizabeth, Countess
of Hereford; Edward II of England.
With his second wife he had Thomas, Earl of Norfolk; Edmund, Earl of Kent.

Edward I, also known as Edward Longshanks and the Hammer of the Scots, was the son of Henry III and Eleanor of Provence. His height and temperament made his contemporaries fearful of him and he is known for establishing parliament as a permanent institution and his cruel behaviour towards the Scots and Jews.

He had assumed more and more control of England in the last years of his father's reign, following his defeat of Simon de Montfort at the Battle of Evesham. On his father's death, he inherited the throne without any opposition even though he was away crusading. He returned to England in 1274 and was crowned on 19 August 1274 at Westminster Abbey.

In Henry III's reign, Llywelyn ap Gruffudd, Prince of Gwynedd, had declared himself Prince of Wales. When Edward came to the throne he demanded that Llywelyn recognise him as overlord and Llywelyn's refusal to do so led to Edward dispatching an army against him in 1277. Llywelyn surrendered and signed the Treaty of Aberconwy, but war broke out again in 1282. Llywelyn was killed in battle and his brother David executed. The 1284 Statute of Rhuddlan saw Wales becoming a principality of England, being governed under English law. Edward spent £80,000 building an "Iron Ring" of castles in Wales to consolidate his control.

In 1290, Edward's wife Eleanor of Castile died. Edward was grief-stricken and erected twelve monuments, known as Eleanor crosses, marking the places her funeral cortège stopped en route to London.

During his reign Edward came into conflict with both Scotland and France. His offer to act as a broker in the Scottish succession crisis in 1291 ended up with him massacring the inhabitants of Berwick, defeating the Scottish forces at Dunbar in 1296 and seizing control of Scotland. He stole the Stone of Scone (the Stone of Destiny or the Scottish coronation stone) and took it to Westminster Abbey. William Wallace led the Scots to victory at Stirling Bridge in 1297 but was defeated at Falkirk in 1298 and eventually captured and executed. Robert the Bruce had himself crowned King of Scotland in 1306 but was defeated by the English at Methven. Bruce was forced into hiding but reappeared in 1307 and began raising support. Edward died of dysentery on 7 July at Burgh-by-Sands, in Cumberland, while travelling north to deal with Bruce. He was buried in Westminster Abbey.

Edward II

1284-1327

Rule: 1307-1327

Marriages: Isabella of France

Issue: Edward III; John of Eltham, Earl of Cornwall; Eleanor of Woodstock;
Joanna of Scotland.

Edward II, or Edward of Caernarfon, was the fourth son of Edward I and Eleanor of Scotland. His reign is seen as disastrous because he did not seem to be interested in ruling the country properly and he alienated people by the favouritism he showed Piers Gaveston, a man who was also rumoured to be Edward's lover (although there is no evidence that Edward was homosexual) and later Hugh Despenser. Gaveston was appointed regent when Edward II travelled to France to marry Isabella of France, Philip IV's daughter.

In 1311, a committee of elected barons known as the Ordainers issued the Ordinances, a manifesto that sought to reform royal finances, limit the king's power and control his actions. One of the requirements of the Ordinances was the exile of Gaveston and other royal favourites from England, Gascony and Ireland. Edward revoked the Ordinances and recalled Gaveston from exile in 1312, which led to Gaveston being seized, tried and executed.

Edward II is known for the defeat of the English by the Scots, led by Robert the Bruce, at the Battle of Bannockburn in June 1314. His unpopularity after Bannockburn was exacerbated by his favouritism of the Despensers: Hugh le Despenser Earl of Winchester, and his son, also called Hugh. The barons called for the Despensers to be exiled and civil war broke out, with the barons, led by the Earls of Lancaster and Hereford, rebelling against Edward. Edward and the Despensers were victorious and Hereford died in battle, while Lancaster was executed. The Ordinances were revoked and Edward took control. However, it was short-lived. Edward's wife, Isabella, was sent to France to negotiate with Charles IV, her brother, but she fell in love with Roger Mortimer, one of the English barons, and instead organised an invasion of England. The Despensers were captured and killed, Edward was taken prisoner and forced to abdicate in favour of his son Edward. Edward II was murdered at Berkeley Castle on 21 September 1327.

Edward III

1312-1377

Rule: 1327-1377

Marriages: Philippa of Hainault.

Issue: 13 children, including Edward the Black Prince; Lionel of Antwerp, Duke of Clarence; John of Gaunt, 1st Duke of Lancaster; Edmund of Langley, 1st Duke of York; Thomas of Woodstock, 1st Duke of Gloucester.

The fourteen-year-old Edward III took over as King of England when his father Edward II abdicated in 1327, and was crowned on 1 February 1327. His mother Isabella acted as regent, helped by her lover Roger Mortimer, until 1330 when Edward rebelled against Mortimer and had him executed, while Isabella was put under house arrest. Edward then assumed control of England in his own right.

There was trouble with Scotland in Edward's reign with English nobles known as "the Disinherited" organising an invasion to reclaim the lands they had lost. Their aim was to replace David II of Scotland with Edward Balliol. With Edward III's support, they were victorious and David was forced into exile. In 1337, Edward's refusal to pay homage to the French king Philip IV led to Philip confiscating Aquitaine from Edward. In response, Edward laid claim to the throne of France and invaded in 1339, sparking a series of wars known as the Hundred Years War. Edward defeated France at the 1346 Battle of Crécy and his son, Edward the Black Prince, was victorious at Poitiers in 1356, capturing John II, King of France. In 1360, Edward agreed to the Treaty of Brétigny, which ended the first phase of the war and saw Edward renouncing his claim to the French throne in return for a large amount of northern and western France. Trouble broke out again in 1369 when Edward's son, John of Gaunt, invaded France, and the Treaty of Bruges meant that England lost most of its territories in France and was left with Calais, Bordeaux and Bayonne.

In contrast to his father, Edward III is known as one of the most successful monarchs of England's Middle Ages. His achievements included legislation like the 1351 Statute of Labourers, the Statutes of Provisors and Praemunire, the Treason Act of 1351, and the development of the existing Parliament with an elected "speaker" representing the Commons. Edward III also created the Order of the Garter in 1348.

Edward's wife Philippa died in 1369 and his mistress Alice Perrers, along with Edward's chamberlain William Latimer, began to dominate the king. Latimer was eventually dismissed and Alice banished, and John of Gaunt began to take control as Edward began to suffer with senility and ill-health. Edward died at Sheen Palace on 21 June 1377 from a stroke. Edward's eldest son, Edward the Black Prince, was already dead, having died in 1376, so the throne was passed to Richard, son of the Black Prince.

Richard II

1367-1400

Rule: 1377-1399

Marriages: Anne of Bohemia; Isabella of Valois.

Issue: None

Richard II was born on 6 January 1367 in Bordeaux and was the son of Edward, the Black Prince, and Joan, 4th Countess of Kent, and the grandson of Edward III. His father died in 1376 so Richard inherited the English throne at the age of ten, when his grandfather died in 1377. He was crowned on 16 July 1377 and a royal council was set up to rule while he was in his minority.

Tensions created by the Black Death and high taxation (the poll tax) led to the Peasants' Revolt of 1381. The courageous fourteen-year-old Richard decided to negotiate with the rebels and he rode out to meet them and their leader Wat Tyler. He agreed to their demands but went back on his word, and the rebellion was put down.

Richard's favouritism of men like Robert de Vere, Earl of Oxford, and Michael de la Pole led to him making powerful enemies. Richard made de la Pole his chancellor in 1383 and raised de Vere to be Duke of Ireland in 1386, causing a lot of resentment. The disaffected magnates formed a group called the Lords Appellant and they persuaded Parliament to impeach de la Pole, threatening to depose the king if he opposed this. Parliament also set up a commission to review and supervise Richard's decisions and actions.

In 1389, Richard assumed power in his own right and in 1397 he took revenge on the lords who had humiliated him in the past. The Earl of Arundel was executed and the others, including Henry of Bolingbroke, son of John of Gaunt, were banished. When Richard travelled to Ireland to deal with a rebellion, Bolingbroke returned to England and laid claim to the throne. Richard was taken prisoner on his return to England and forced to abdicate on 30 September 1399. Bolingbroke was crowned king on 13 October 1399. Richard died on 14 February 1400 while he was imprisoned at Pontefract Castle. It is unclear whether his death was murder. His body was put on display at Old St Paul's Cathedral before being buried at Kings Langley Church. He was reburied at Westminster Abbey in 1413 by Henry V.

Henry IV

1366-1413

Rule: 1399-1413

Marriages: Mary de Bohun; Joanna (Joan) of Navarre.

Issue: Henry V; Thomas of Lancaster, 1st Duke of Clarence;
John of Lancaster, 1st Duke of Bedford; Humphrey, 1st Duke of Gloucester;
Blanche, Electress Palatine; Philippa, Queen of Denmark - all by his first wife.

Henry IV was known as Henry of Bolingbroke because he was born at Bolingbroke Castle in Lincolnshire. He was the son of John of Gaunt, 1st Duke of Lancaster, and his first wife Blanche, and was the grandson of Edward III.

After Richard II prevented Henry from inheriting his father's lands in 1399, Henry raised support for himself against Richard and deposed the king. Henry seized the throne and was crowned king on 13 October 1399. Due to his usurpation of the throne, Henry had to deal with many revolts and rebellions during his reign, including an uprising by Owain Glyndwr in Wales, which started in 1400 when Glyndwr proclaimed himself Prince of Wales and challenged English rule; rebellions led by the Percys and Mortimers; and a northern rebellion led by Richard le Scrope, Archbishop of York. Henry was able to hang on to his throne but became increasingly unpopular after his 1403 marriage to Joanna of Navarre, who many believed to be a witch, and the execution of Scrope in 1405.

From around 1405, Henry began to suffer with ill-health, which consisted of a severe skin disorder and attacks that may have been epilepsy or strokes. A prophecy had told how the king would die in Jerusalem, which Henry took to mean as him dying on crusade in the Holy Lands, but he died in Jerusalem Chamber, a room in the abbot's house of Westminster Abbey, on 20 March 1413. He was buried in Canterbury Cathedral.

Henry V

1387-1422

Rule: 1413-1422

Marriages: Catherine of Valois, daughter of Charles VI of France.

Issue: Henry VI.

Henry V was born on 16 September 1387 at Monmouth Castle and was the eldest son of Henry IV and his first wife Mary de Bohun. Henry V is best known for his famous victory against the French at the Battle of Agincourt and for the hero he is in Shakespeare's famous play.

Henry rose to prominence in his father's reign, campaigning against the rebels in Owen Glyndwr's rebellions in the early 1400s, fighting at the Battle of Shrewsbury against Harry "Hotspur" Percy and receiving a serious arrow wound to the face, and taking on more responsibility as his father's health declined.

Henry became king on his father's death in March 1413 and was crowned at Westminster Abbey on 9 April 1413. Trouble soon erupted with the Lollard uprising of 1414, but Henry quickly suppressed it. He then concentrated on laying claim to the throne of France, going to war against Charles VI, who was suffering from mental illness. He departed England for France in August 1415 and was able to capture Harfleur on 22 September. On 25 October 1415, the skill of the English archers enabled Henry's smaller army to defeat the French force and win the historic Battle of Agincourt.

His victory led to alliances with Emperor Sigismund and the Duke of Burgundy, and by 1419 Henry had gained control of Normandy and Picardy. The Treaty of Troyes was signed between Henry and Charles VI in May 1420, in which it was agreed that Henry would marry Charles' daughter Catherine de Valois and that Henry's heirs would inherit the French throne on the death of Charles. Unfortunately, Henry became ill at the siege of Mieux in May 1422, after successfully capturing it, and died of "camp fever" on 31 August 1422 at Bois de Vincennes. He was buried at Westminster Abbey.

Henry VI

1421-1471

Rule: 1422-1461, 1470-1471.

Marriages: Margaret of Anjou.

Issue: Edward, Prince of Wales.

Henry VI was born on 6 December 1421 at Windsor Castle and was the son of Henry V and Catherine of Valois. He was just nine months old when he inherited the throne of England and eleven months old when he became King of France. He was the youngest monarch to inherit the throne of England and a regency council, headed by his uncles, Humphrey Duke of Gloucester and John Duke of Bedford, and half-uncle Cardinal Henry Beaufort, Bishop of Winchester, ruled while he was in his minority. Henry was crowned in Westminster Abbey on 6 November 1429 and crowned King of France at Notre Dame, Paris, in 1431.

In 1437, at the age of fifteen, Henry was deemed old enough to rule in his own right, but he was dominated by stronger personalities at court. In 1445, Henry married Margaret of Anjou, the niece of Charles VII, by the terms of the Treaty of Tours, which saw Henry agree to give Maine and Anjou to Charles. This agreement led to trouble between the Duke of Suffolk, who backed Henry, and Humphrey Duke of Gloucester, who was pro-war with France. Gloucester was charged with treason and imprisoned.

By 1450, England had lost Normandy and Aquitaine to France and these losses, combined with the fact that the returning soldiers had not been paid, led to a rebellion in Kent led by Jack Cade, a supporter of Richard Duke of York. It achieved nothing but in 1452 York raised an army and demanded the removal of the Duke of Somerset from government. Henry agreed, but the queen supported Somerset and York failed.

In August 1453, Henry VI suffered a complete mental breakdown. York assumed control, becoming regent, and imprisoned Somerset in the Tower of London. However, Henry made a partial recovery at Christmas 1454 and York became alienated. Further attacks of mental illness and the struggle between York and Margaret of Anjou led to the civil war that has become known as the Wars of the Roses. Somerset was killed at the First Battle of St Albans in May 1455 and York was killed in December 1460. Henry was deposed in 1461 by Edward of York, York's son, who declared himself king in March 1461 and who defeated the Lancastrians at the Battle of Towton. Henry and Margaret were able to escape to Scotland, but Henry was captured and imprisoned in the Tower of London in 1465.

In October 1470, Henry was restored to the throne and Edward IV forced into exile. It was to be a short-lived restoration. Edward IV was victorious at the Battle of Tewkesbury, where Henry's son, Edward, was killed. Henry was imprisoned once more in the Tower and he died on 21 May 1471. It was said that he died of melancholy, but it is now believed that he was stabbed to death on the orders of Edward IV. He was buried at Chertsey Abbey but moved by Richard III to St George's Chapel, Windsor Castle.

Edward IV

1442-1483

Rule: 1461-1470, 1471-1483

Marriages: Elizabeth Woodville

Issue: Elizabeth of York; Mary; Cecily; Edward V; Margaret; Richard; Anne; George; Catherine; Bridget. Also a number of illegitimate children.

Edward IV was born on 28 April 1442 at Rouen and was the son of Richard, Duke of York, and Cecily Neville, and was descended from Edward III through Edward's second son Lionel, Duke of Clarence. He became King of England after deposing the Lancastrian king Henry VI twice with the support of his cousin Richard Neville, Earl of Warwick, who was known as "The Kingmaker".

Edward angered the Earl of Warwick by marrying Elizabeth Woodville, widow of Sir John Grey of Groby, in secret in 1464, ruining Warwick's plans for a marriage alliance with France. He alienated Warwick further by advancing members of Elizabeth's family and Warwick turned to Edward's brother George, Duke of Clarence, for support. In 1469, Warwick and Clarence led an army against Edward and defeated him at the Battle of Edgecote Moor on 26 July. The queen's father and one of her brothers were captured and executed, and Edward was captured at Olney. Warwick lacked support to rule as king and was forced to release Edward. Warwick and Clarence fled to France where they made an alliance with Margaret of Anjou, wife of Henry VI, agreeing to invade England and restore Henry VI to the throne. Henry was restored as king in October 1470, but Edward was able to gain the support of his brother-in-law Charles, Duke of Burgundy, and returned to England with his brother Richard, Duke of Gloucester, and an army. He was able to win support in England and marched to London, where he took Henry VI captive. He defeated and killed the Earl of Warwick at the Battle of Barnet and the Lancastrian forces at the Battle of Tewkesbury. Clarence was accused of plotting against Edward in 1477 and was put to death, allegedly by being drowned in a butt of malmsey wine, in 1478.

The last years of his reign were ones of peace and prosperity. Edward died suddenly on 9 April 1483 at Westminster but was able to name his brother, Richard of Gloucester, Protector of England while his son was too young to reign in his own right. He was buried in St George's Chapel, Windsor Castle.

Edward V

1470-1483

Rule: 9 April 1483 – 26 June 1483

Marriages: Did not marry.

Issue: None

Edward V was born on 2 November 1470, while his mother was in sanctuary in Westminster Abbey, and was the eldest son of Edward IV and his wife Elizabeth Woodville. He was created Prince of Wales in June 1471 and sent to Ludlow Castle in the Welsh Marches in 1473 as notional president of the Council of Wales and the Marches. He was raised there by his uncle Anthony, Earl Rivers.

Edward was just twelve when his father died and he inherited the throne. Rivers was escorting the boy king to London when they were intercepted by Richard, Duke of Gloucester, who had been appointed as Protector by Edward IV. Rivers and Sir Richard Grey were taken prisoner and then executed in June 1483. Edward was taken to the Tower of London to prepare for his coronation, and was joined there by his brother Richard. Gloucester then claimed that the princes were illegitimate because Edward IV had been pre-contracted to marry Eleanor Butler before his marriage to Elizabeth Woodville, thus making his marriage to Elizabeth invalid. On 26 June 1483, Gloucester was proclaimed King Richard III.

It is not known what happened to Edward V and his brother, who have gone down in history as "the Princes in the Tower". They disappeared but two skeletons were found in the Tower of London in 1674 and later examination, in the 1930s, found them to be of two children of about the same ages as the princes. The skeletons were buried in Westminster Abbey.

Richard III

1452-1485

Rule: 1483-1485

Marriages: Anne Neville, daughter of Richard Neville, 16th Earl of Warwick.

Issue: Edward of Middleham; 2 illegitimate children: John of Gloucester; Katherine Plantagenet.

Richard III was born on 2 October 1452 at Fotheringhay Castle and was the youngest son of Richard, Duke of York, and Cecily Neville, daughter of the Earl of Westmorland. He became king after deposing his nephew Edward V in June 1483 and was crowned on 6 July 1483 at Westminster Abbey.

In September 1483, Henry Stafford, Duke of Buckingham, led a rebellion against Richard with the intention of deposing him and putting Henry Tudor, Earl of Richmond, on the throne. The rebellion was quashed and Buckingham was executed. However, Henry Tudor, who was in exile in Brittany, landed at Milford Haven, in Wales, on 7 August 1485 with a force of his English supporters and French mercenaries.

Richard and his forces met Henry's on 22 August 1485 near Market Bosworth in Leicestershire at the Battle of Bosworth. Although Henry had managed to build an army of around 5,000 men, Richard's men are thought to have numbered around 12,000. Richard must have felt confident that he could squash Henry, particularly when they finally met and Henry's men were struggling to negotiate marshland and Richard's men were on higher ground. Richard and his army certainly had the advantage, particularly as Henry had no battle experience. Richard took the initiative and sent the Duke of Norfolk and some men out to attack Henry's men, who had become strung out in a line below them after being forced to circle around the marsh. Fortunately for Henry, he had the Earl of Oxford, an experienced soldier, on his side, who knew just what to do. Oxford quickly created a wedge of men between two banners and, in the fighting that followed, the Duke of Norfolk was killed. Things looked good for the king until the Stanleys, who had been watching events unfold but had not committed their armies to any particular side, made a decision. As Richard III's cavalry clashed with Henry and his men, who had been on their way to appeal to the Stanleys, William Stanley ordered his men to attack the king and his cavalry. Before the Stanleys and their men reached Henry and Richard, Richard's men managed to kill Henry's standard bearer Sir William Brandon, and unhorse Sir John Cheyne, but the tide turned when Stanley's men reached the spot. King Richard III, himself, was killed and Henry Tudor was crowned King Henry VII later that day when Richard's crown was recovered.

Richard was buried in the choir of the Grey Friars monastery. Human remains were found in an archaeological dig in a Leicester car park in 2012 and DNA results proved that "beyond reasonable doubt" the remains were Richard III. The skeleton showed that the king had suffered from a scoliosis of the spine and that a large wound to the base of the skull, probably from a halberd, and a blow from a bladed weapon had killed him. His remains were reinterred at Leicester Cathedral.

Henry VII

1457-1509

Rule: 1485-1509

Marriages: Elizabeth of York, daughter of Edward IV.

Issue: Arthur, Prince of Wales; Margaret (consort of James IV of Scotland); Henry VIII; Elizabeth; Mary, Queen of France; Edmund, Duke of Somerset; Katherine.
Only Arthur, Margaret, Henry and Mary survived childhood.

Henry VII, or Henry Tudor, was born on 28 January 1457 at Pembroke Castle and was the son of Edmund Tudor, 1st Earl of Richmond, and Margaret Beaufort. Henry's paternal grandparents were Owen Tudor (a former page to Henry V) and Catherine of Valois, the widow of Henry V and mother of Henry VI. His maternal grandfather was John Beaufort, 1st Duke of Somerset, and his maternal great-grandfather (John Beaufort, 1st Earl of Somerset) was a son of John of Gaunt, 1st Duke of Lancaster, and his mistress (and later wife), Katherine Swynford. It was from this Beaufort side of the family that Henry VII derived his claim to the throne. Lady Margaret Beaufort was only thirteen years old when Henry was born and already a widow, his father having died from the plague three months earlier while imprisoned by Yorkists. Margaret had been taken in by her brother-in-law, Jasper Tudor, Earl of Pembroke, the man who helped bring Henry up, who took him into exile in Brittany and who helped him win the crown of England.

Henry VII was the first Tudor monarch and he claimed the throne after defeating Richard III at the Battle of Bosworth Field on 22 August 1485. On 18 January 1486, he united the Houses of Lancaster and York by marrying Elizabeth of York, daughter of Edward IV, a move that strengthened his monarchy and his future offsprings' claims to the throne. The marriage between Henry and Elizabeth was happy and successful, but Elizabeth died on her birthday in 1503 at the age of thirty-seven. She died from a post-partum infection and her husband was said to have been devastated. He had lost his eldest son Arthur in 1502.

Henry VII ruled for over twenty-three years and died on 21 April 1509, aged fifty-two, at Richmond Palace. He was buried in the Henry VII Chapel at Westminster Abbey with his wife Elizabeth of York. His achievements include securing the throne and passing his crown unchallenged on to his son and heir Henry VIII; uniting the kingdom and bringing peace to England after decades of unrest; reforming and modernising government and the legal system, for example, establishing the Court of the Star Chamber; and restoring the crown's fortunes.

Henry VIII

1491-1547

Rule: 1509-1547

Marriages: Catherine of Aragon (annulled); Anne Boleyn (executed for alleged treason); Jane Seymour (died after childbirth); Anne of Cleves (annulled); Catherine Howard (executed for alleged treason); Catherine Parr (outlived him).

Issue: By Catherine of Aragon: Henry, Duke of Cornwall (died in infancy); Mary I. By Anne Boleyn: Elizabeth I. By Jane Seymour: Edward VI. By his mistress Elizabeth Blount: illegitimate son Henry Fitzroy, Duke of Richmond and Somerset, who died at the age of seventeen.

Henry VIII was born on 28 June 1491 at Greenwich Palace. He was the second son of Henry VII and Elizabeth of York, but became heir to the throne when his brother, Arthur, died in 1502. He inherited the throne on the death of his father in April 1509 when he was just seventeen years old, and he was crowned on 24 June 1509 in a joint coronation with his new bride Catherine of Aragon, the widow of his brother.

His reign was seen as the start of a new era, after his father's harsh regime, and Henry was very much a Renaissance prince at the start, with his charm, good looks, intelligence, love of sport and desire to fight bribery and corruption. However, he has gone down in history as a larger than life, hulk of a man who had six wives, who executed two of them, and who, according to one contemporary source, executed 72,000 during his reign. His reign is famous for the break with Rome, which happened as a result of Henry VIII's "Great Matter", his quest for an annulment of his marriage to his first wife Catherine of Aragon. Catherine had been unable to provide Henry with a living son and Henry had come to view the marriage as contrary to God's laws, since Catherine was his brother's widow. He had also fallen in love with Anne Boleyn. The pope refused to grant Henry an annulment, but Henry took matters into his own hands after reading that kings and princes were only answerable to God. The marriage was annulled in 1533, Henry VIII married Anne Boleyn and the Reformation Parliament of 1529-1536 passed the main pieces of legislation that led to the break with Rome and the English Reformation.

His achievements included the founding of the English Navy; the foundation of the Church of England after the break with Rome; his patronage of the Arts and his bringing the Renaissance to England; the establishment of the Kingdom of Ireland; his remodelling of government and taxation; his promotion of Parliament; the translation of the Bible into English; his major building programme; and the passing of the crown to his son Edward without opposition.

Henry VIII died on 28 January 1547 at the Palace of Whitehall. He was buried with his third wife, Jane Seymour, in St George's Chapel, Windsor Castle.

Edward VI

1537-1553

Rule: 1547-1553

Marriages: Did not marry.

Issue: None

Edward VI was born on 12 October 1537 at Hampton Court Palace. He was the son of Henry VIII and his third wife, Jane Seymour, who died twelve days after giving birth to him, probably of puerperal fever. He was tutored by scholars such as John Cheke, Richard Cox, Roger Ascham and Jean Belmain, and it appears that he was an intelligent child. By the age of twelve he was undertaking work on religious issues and controversies and had written a treatise about the Pope being the Antichrist.

Henry VIII died on 28 January 1547, making Edward King Edward VI of England. Edward was only nine years old and far too young to rule over the country himself so a Council of Regency was set up, according to Henry VIII's will. Sixteen executors had been named by Henry to act as a regency council until Edward came of age. The council members had been appointed as equals, but Edward's uncle, Edward Seymour, took the lead and became Lord Protector of the Realm. Seymour was not content with just being Lord Protector. He convinced the young king to sign letters patent giving him the right to appoint members of his choosing to the Privy Council and to only consult them when he himself chose to.

Seymour was a staunch Protestant and so teamed up with Thomas Cranmer, Archbishop of Canterbury, to make the necessary changes to make England a fully Protestant country. His radical reforms, combined with the country's economic problems, led to social unrest in 1548 and 1549, and his council rose against him. Seymour was arrested and by February 1550 John Dudley, Earl of Warwick, was heading the Regency Council. Seymour was later executed for plotting to overthrow Dudley. Although John Dudley did not take on the title of Lord Protector, he was the most important political figure in the country and virtually ruled England.

By the winter of 1552/1553 it was obvious that Edward VI was seriously ill. Fearing the succession of a Catholic monarch who would undo all of the religious reforms of his reign, Edward wrote his "devise for the succession", naming Lady Jane Grey as his heir and removing his half-sisters from the succession. He died on 6 July 1553 at Greenwich Palace. The exact cause of his death is unknown, although theories include tuberculosis and bronchopneumonia.

Jane

1537-1554

Rule: 6 July 1553 to 19 July 1553

Marriages: Guildford Dudley, son of John Dudley, Duke of Northumberland.

Issue: None

Queen Jane, commonly known as Lady Jane Grey, was born in 1537 (May or October) at Bradgate Park in Leicestershire. She was the eldest daughter of Henry Grey, Duke of Suffolk, and Frances Brandon, who was the daughter of Charles Brandon Duke of Suffolk and Mary Tudor, Queen of France. She was an intelligent girl and received a top-class education. Her main tutor was John Aylmer but she also met the top scholars of the day during her time living with Thomas Seymour, as his ward, and his wife Dowager Queen Catherine Parr. She also met famous reformists and humanists. She loved Greek and was a linguist with a knowledge of Latin and Hebrew, on top of the usual modern languages.

In May 1553, Jane married Guildford Dudley, son of John Dudley, Duke of Northumberland, Edward VI's chief adviser. It was a triple marriage – Jane's sister married Lord Herbert and Guildford's sister, Catherine, married Lord Hastings. Before his death in July 1553, Edward VI wrote his "devise for the Succession", removing his half-sisters Mary and Elizabeth from the succession and naming Lady Jane Grey as his heir. Edward VI died on the 6 July 1553 and on the 7 July the Mayor of London and other city officials were called to Greenwich to swear an oath of allegiance to Queen Jane. Jane was proclaimed queen on 10 July but Mary had already proclaimed herself as queen at her home in Norfolk and was busy raising support. On 19 July the Earls of Pembroke and Arundel persuaded the privy council to swap sides from Jane to Mary and Mary was proclaimed queen. Jane and Guildford were arrested.

On 13 November 1553, Guildford and Jane were found guilty of high treason and sentenced to death. It was thought, however, that Mary would spare Jane's life. The nail in Jane's coffin was Wyatt's Rebellion of January 1554. Although Jane was not involved in any way, her father, the Duke of Suffolk, was involved and Jane was used as a figurehead. Mary was then pressurised by her husband, Philip of Spain, to get rid of Jane, who could be used again as a focus of rebellion. Jane and Guildford were executed on 12 February 1554 and laid to rest in the Chapel of St Peter ad Vincula, Tower of London.

Although Jane is often referred to as "The Nine Days Queen" she actually reigned for thirteen days, from Edward's death on 6 July to when Mary I was proclaimed queen on 19 July.

Mary I

1516-1558

Rule: 1553-1558

Marriages: Philip II of Spain.

Issue: None

Mary was born on 18 February 1516 at Greenwich Palace and was the daughter of Henry VIII and his first wife Catherine of Aragon. She was an intelligent girl, was known as a linguist and loved music and dancing. Mary was made illegitimate and removed from the succession after the annulment of her father's marriage to Catherine of Aragon in 1533 and the subsequent birth of her half-sister Elizabeth, daughter of Henry VIII and Anne Boleyn. She and Elizabeth (who had been removed from the succession in 1536 after the fall of her mother) were restored to the line of succession, after their half-brother Edward, by Parliament in 1543, but Edward VI chose to remove his half-sisters from the succession as he lay dying in 1553 and chose Lady Jane Grey as his heir. Mary was forced to fight for the throne and was proclaimed queen on 19 July 1553.

Mary sought to bring England back to Rome by repealing all of the Protestant legislation of Edward VI's reign. She also introduced an act undoing the annulment of her parents' marriage and making it valid. She married Philip of Spain on 25 July 1554 at Winchester Cathedral. On 18 September 1554, it was announced at the Imperial Court that Mary I was pregnant but it turned out to be a false pregnancy. Later, in 1557, it was thought that the queen was pregnant but it was another false alarm.

Although Mary's reign has often been seen as a disaster, in comparison to Elizabeth I's "Golden Age", Mary achieved much during her short reign. She preserved the Tudor succession; she strengthened the position of Parliament by using it for her religious settlement; she established the "gender free" authority of the crown; she restored and strengthened the administrative structure of the church; and she maintained the navy and reformed the militia. Mary was also the first queen regnant of England.

Mary has gone down in history as the monarch who lost Calais, and as "Bloody Mary", due to the burnings of Protestants during her reign. Mary died on 17 November 1558 at St James's Palace. Her health had been declining for some time and she contracted a fever in August 1558 and then "dropsy" in the October. She was laid to rest at Westminster Abbey.

Elizabeth I

1533-1603

Rule: 1558-1603

Marriages: Did not marry.

Issue: None

Although Elizabeth supported her half-sister Mary when she claimed the throne in July 1553, she was taken to the Tower of London on 18 March 1554 after being charged with being involved in Wyatt's Rebellion. She was released on 19 May 1554 and placed under house arrest at Woodstock. In April 1555 she was summoned to court to attend Mary I who was, allegedly, pregnant. After spending a few months with Mary, she was finally given permission to leave court for Hatfield, her own estate, on 18 March 1555.

Elizabeth inherited the throne from her childless half-sister on 17 November 1558. She ruled England for forty-four years and made a huge difference to the country. England was in a depressing state when she inherited it from Mary I, yet when Elizabeth died England was a strong and prosperous country, a force to be reckoned with, and that is why her reign is known as "The Golden Age". Her main achievements include defeating the Spanish Armada, following on from her father's work on the navy, and turning England into a strong and dominant naval power, defending England from Scotland and actually turning the Scots into a permanent ally, increasing literacy in England, expanding England overseas by encouraging explorers like Sir Walter Raleigh, Sir Francis Drake, and Sir John Hawkins to discover new places and form colonies, founding the Church of England as we know it today, raising the status of England abroad, surviving and defeating plots and uprisings against her, helping the poor by her poor laws, ruling England in her own right as queen without a consort, and promoting the arts – her love of arts led to theatres being built and great poets and playwrights like Shakespeare, Spenser and Marlow emerging.

Elizabeth I died on 24 March 1603 and was buried at Westminster Abbey in the vault of her grandfather Henry VII. She was moved in 1606 to her present resting place, a tomb in the Lady Chapel of Westminster Abbey which she shares with her half-sister Mary I. King James I spent over £11,000 on Elizabeth I's lavish funeral and he also arranged for a white marble monument to be built. The tomb is inscribed with the words "Consorts both in throne and grave, here we rest two sisters, Elizabeth and Mary, in hope of our resurrection."

She is known as the Virgin Queen, Gloriana and Good Queen Bess.

James I

1566-1625

Rule: 1603-1625

Marriages: Anne of Denmark.

Issue: 7 children, but only three survived childhood: Henry, Prince of Wales; Elizabeth, Queen of Bohemia; Charles I.

James I was born on 19 June 1566 at Edinburgh Castle. He was the only son of Mary, Queen of Scots, and her second husband Henry Stuart, Lord Darnley, and both his parents were descended from Margaret Tudor, daughter of Henry VII. James became King James VI of Scotland in 1567, at the age of just thirteen months, on the abdication of his mother. Regents ruled Scotland until he reached his majority. His mother was executed in 1587 after being implicated in plots against Elizabeth I.

James married Anne of Denmark, the second daughter of King Frederick II of Denmark, in 1589. He succeeded Elizabeth I at her death on 24 March 1603 because she died without issue. James used the title King of Great Britain because he ruled over England, Scotland and Ireland until his death. His reign started well for Catholics, with James limiting the restrictions on Catholics, but things took a turn for the worse when, after opposition from Protestants, James reversed his policy less than a year after implementing it. The Catholics' hopes were dashed and they felt betrayed. One party of young Catholics, headed by Robert Catesby, decided to seek revenge through rebellion. They met in London in May 1604 and hatched a plan, now known as the Gunpowder Plot, to blow up the Palace of Westminster, on the opening session of Parliament, thus killing the king, the Royal family, members of Parliament, the Lords and the leading bishops. This would be the first step in their rebellion, which sought to replace James I with his daughter, Princess Elizabeth, as a Catholic queen. The plot looked as if it would be successful until Lord Monteagle received an anonymous tip-off. The cellars beneath Westminster were searched on the night of the 4/5 November and Guy Fawkes was caught with thirty-six barrels of gunpowder. On 5 November 1605, Londoners were encouraged to celebrate the king's narrow escape by lighting bonfires around the city. This celebration is remembered in the UK every year.

James I is also known for continuing Elizabeth's "Golden Age" of literature and drama; for writing his own works (*Daemonologie, The True Lawe of Free Monarchies, Basilikon Doron* and *A Counterblaste to Tobacco*); for the King James Bible; for his interest in witchcraft and subsequent witch hunts; and for enjoying the affection of his people. He is also known for his close relationship with George Villiers, who he created Duke of Buckingham.

In his fifties, James was plagued with ill-health, suffering with gout, arthritis and kidney problems. He suffered a stroke and died on 27 March 1625 at Theobald's House near Cheshunt. He was buried at Westminster Abbey.

Charles I

1600-1649 and the English Civil War

Rule: 1625-1649

Marriages: Henrietta Maria, daughter of Henry IV of France.

Issue: 9 children, including Charles II; Mary, Princess Royal (married William II, Prince of Orange); James II; Henry, Duke of Gloucester; Henrietta Anne (married Philip, Duke of Orléans).

Charles I was born on 19 November 1600 at Dunfermline Palace, Fife, Scotland, and was the second son of James VI of Scotland (James I of England) and Anne of Denmark. He succeeded to the throne in 1625, at the age of twenty-five, on the death of his father. After a failed match with the Spanish Infanta , he married sixteen-year-old Henrietta Maria, daughter of Henry IV of France, in 1625. Charles was crowned at Westminster Abbey on 2 February 1626. Although the first years of their marriage were marked by quarrels, the couple grew to like each other and, after losing a baby boy in 1629, Henrietta gave Charles a living son in 1630, the future Charles II.

Charles's belief in the divine right of kings and absolute monarchy led to him being perceived as a tyrant. His religious and financial policies, his wars with Spain and France, his stubbornness, his reliance on his favourite Buckingham, and the way he ruled without Parliament, in a period known by his enemies as the Eleven Years' Tyranny (1629 to 1640), led to civil war and his downfall. He was forced to recall Parliament in April 1640 to raise money to put down rebellion in Scotland, but dissolved it just weeks later due to members wanting to air their grievances. Parliament met again in November 1640, in a session known as the Long Parliament, and moved to impeach key royal advisers and then passed the Grand Remonstrance, a list of abuses of power committed by Charles's ministers. In response, he accused 5 members of the Commons of treason and entered the House of Commons on 4 January 1642 with an armed guard to arrest them. The men had already fled.

On 22 August 1642, Charles raised the royal standard at Nottingham, calling for his subjects to support him against rebellion. The first real battle of the Civil War was at Edgehill in October 1642 and the battles over the next two years were inconclusive, until the Battle of Marston Moor in July 1644, when the Parliamentarians won. On 14 June 1645, at the Battle of Naseby, the Royalist forces were again defeated by the Parliamentarians and in May 1646 Charles gave himself to the Scottish Presbyterian army. He was handed over to Parliament in January 1647 and then imprisoned in Carisbrooke Castle. Charles was able to negotiate with the Scots, who agreed to invade England in an attempt to restore him. The Scots were defeated in August 1648 at the Battle of Preston and Royalist uprisings were quelled by the Parliamentarians. Parliament was purged of those with Royalist sympathies and the Rump Parliament indicted Charles for high treason. Charles was found guilty and condemned to death on 26 January 1649 and beheaded on a scaffold in front of Banqueting House, Whitehall, on 30 January 1649. He was buried in the same vault at Henry VIII in St George's Chapel, Windsor Castle, on 9 February 1649.

The Interregnum

1649-1660

The interregnum was the period between Charles I's execution and the restoration of the monarchy, when his son became King Charles II in May 1660. The Interregnum actually consisted of two periods: the Commonwealth (1649-53) and the Protectorate (1653-9).

Following the downfall and execution of Charles I in January 1649, an act to abolish the monarchy was voted on and then passed by the Rump Parliament on 17 March 1649, with the House of Lords being abolished two days later. On 19 May 1649, an act was passed making England "a Commonwealth and Free-State" governed by "The Representatives of the People in Parliament". On 20 April 1653, Oliver Cromwell, a Puritan, member of Parliament and a military commander who had fought against the Royalists, marched into the House of Commons with around forty musketeers and forced the dissolution of the Rump Parliament. Between July and December 1653, an assembly of men nominated by Cromwell, and known as the Barebones Parliament, ruled the country, but divisions led to its dismissal in December 1653. A new constitution called the Instrument of Government was drawn up by Major-General John Lambert and this made Cromwell Lord Protector.

Cromwell refused the crown but did agree to name his successor, and when he died in September 1658 his son Richard became Lord Protector. Richard served as Protector for only a few months because, unlike his father, he did not have the confidence of the army. In May 1659, Richard resigned as Lord Protector and the Commonwealth was re-established. In April 1660, General George Monck sent a message to Charles I's son Charles, who was in exile in France, offering him the crown. On 8 May, Parliament proclaimed Charles II as king.

Charles II

1630-1685

Rule: 1660-1685

Marriages: Catherine of Braganza.

Issue: No legitimate children, but he had around 12 illegitimate children including James, Duke of Monmouth.

Charles II was born on 29 May 1630 at St James's Palace in London and was the son of Charles I and Henrietta Marie of France. He was crowned King of England on 23 April 1661 after the monarchy was restored and he was invited to return to England from exile in April 1660. Although his reign is taken as starting in 1660, Parliament proclaimed that Charles had actually been the lawful monarch since his father's execution in January 1649.

On his acceptance of General Monck's invitation for Charles to return to England as king, Charles made the Declaration of Breda in which he issued a general pardon for crimes committed during the Civil War and Interregnum by those who now acknowledged him as king. It was a fresh start.

Charles II has gone down in history as the "Merry Monarch" who brought joy back to the country after the austerities of the Puritan Oliver Cromwell's protectorate. But as well as being witty and tolerant he is also known for his licentious court, his collection of mistresses (his nickname was "Old Rowley", after one of the stallions in the royal stud) and his failed foreign policies. While his reign saw the rise of the arts and science - with Charles supporting the newly founded Royal Society by royal charter and acting as patron to Christopher Wren, the architect responsible for St Paul's Cathedral - it was also marked by the Great Plague in 1665, the Great Fire in 1666 and religious divisions. Widespread anti-Catholic hysteria resulted from the Popish Plot of 1678, which was eventually found to be fictitious but was believed to be an attempt by Jesuits to assassinate Charles and replace him with his Catholic brother James.

Charles II died on 6 February 1685 at Whitehall in London following a stroke suffered on 2 February. He converted to Catholicism on his deathbed and was buried in Westminster Abbey.

James II

1633-1701

Rule: 1685-1689

Marriages: Anne Hyde; Mary of Modena.

Issue: By Anne Hyde: 4 sons and 4 daughters, including Mary II and Queen Anne.
The others died in infancy. By Mary of Modena: 2 sons and 5 daughters, but
only James Prince of Wales and Louisa Maria Teresa survived infancy.
James also had illegitimate children by his mistresses Arabella Churchill
(including James Fitzjames, Duke of Berwick) and Catherine Sedley.

James was born on 14 October 1633 at St James's Palace, London, and was the second surviving son of Charles I and Henrietta Maria of France. He inherited the throne on the death of his brother Charles II, who died without a legitimate heir. He ruled England and Ireland as James II and Scotland as James VII. He was crowned on 23 April 1685 at Westminster Abbey in a joint coronation ceremony with his second wife Mary.

James had converted to Catholicism while he and his first wife, Anne, were in exile in France, but he had to go public about his faith in 1673 when the Test Act required all those in public office to take an oath denouncing Catholic practices and to take Anglican communion. Although anti-Catholic hysteria resulting from the Popish Plot in 1678 threatened his chance of succession, he was able to accede to the throne without opposition. Trouble reared its ugly head soon in June 1685, with James's Protestant nephew James, Duke of Monmouth, landing at Lyme Regis in Dorset and proclaiming himself king. Monmouth was defeated and captured at the Battle of Sedgemoor and executed on 15 July 1685.

Although James issued the Declaration of Indulgence in 1687, which granted religious freedom within the British Isles, James made himself unpopular by his promotion of Catholics in government and by his prosecution of seven Anglican bishops, including the Archbishop of Canterbury, in 1688 after they refused to read out the Declaration of Indulgence from the pulpit. This, combined with the birth of a Catholic son and heir to James and his wife Mary in June 1688, caused seven English noblemen, "the Immortal Seven", to write to William of Orange, James's son-in-law, and investigate claims that the new baby prince was an impostor. William and his forces landed in Devon on 5 November 1688 and began their march to London – this was the Glorious Revolution. James fled to France and it was declared that he had abdicated as king. The crown was offered to James's daughter, Mary, to rule jointly with her husband William of Orange.

James attempted to regain the throne in 1690, with the support of Louis XIV of France and forces built up in Ireland, but was defeated by William at the Battle of the Boyne. He fled once more to France and spent his last years in the royal château of Saint-Germain-en-Laye, where he died on 6 September 1701. He was buried in the Church of the English Benedictines in Paris.

William III & Mary II

1650-1702 & 1662-1694

Rule: 1689-1702

Marriages: William and Mary married in 1677.

Issue: None

William III was born on 4 November 1650 at The Hague and was the only child of William II, Prince of Orange, and Mary, daughter of Charles I. His father died when he was just a few days old and William became Prince of Orange. He became Stadtholder of the United Provinces of the Netherlands in 1672.

Mary II was born on 30 April 1662 at St James's Palace, London, and was the eldest daughter of James II and his first wife Anne Hyde. Although her father converted to Catholicism, Mary was brought up a Protestant. William and Mary married at St James's Palace on 4 November 1677 and William took Mary back to the United Provinces.

In 1688, following the Glorious Revolution against her father James II, Mary was offered the crown as queen regnant. Mary refused, not wanting her husband to have to defer to her, and so Parliament offered the couple the throne as joint sovereigns. They were crowned at Westminster Abbey on 21 April 1689. They also accepted the throne of Scotland on 11 May 1689.

The Convention Parliament, which had declared the abdication of James II, made William and Mary accept a Bill of Rights before installing them as king and queen. This bill established constitutional monarchy by limiting the power of the crown and setting out the rights and liberties of Parliament and the subject. It established freedom of speech in Parliament and forbade monarchs from taxing subjects without Parliament's consent, maintaining a standing army in peace time without Parliament's consent and dispensing or suspending laws without Parliament's consent. The Bill also named William and Mary as James II's successors and settled the succession on the heirs of Mary, her sister Anne, and William, thus ensuring a Protestant succession.

Mary died childless of smallpox at Kensington Palace on 28 December 1694 and was buried at Westminster Abbey on 5 March 1695. Although their marriage had appeared unhappy at the start, William was devastated by Mary's death. By 1701, William was still childless, having not re-married, and Anne's heir had died, so Parliament passed the Act of Settlement in which it settled the succession on Princess Sophia, Electress of Hanover, granddaughter of James I, and her heirs. William died of pneumonia, following a fall from his horse caused by it stumbling into a molehill, on 8 March 1702 and was laid to rest next to his wife in Westminster Abbey.

Anne

1665-1714

Rule: 1702-1714

Marriages: Prince George of Denmark

Issue: Anne was pregnant 17 times but the majority of her pregnancies resulted in miscarriages or stillbirths. She had 5 live births (Mary; Anne Sophia; William; Mary; George), but only William, Duke of Gloucester, survived infancy, and he died at the age of 11.

Anne was born on 6 February 1665 at St James's Palace and was the fourth child of James II and his first wife Anne Hyde. Like her elder sister Mary, she was brought up a Protestant on the orders of her uncle, Charles II. She married Prince George of Denmark, brother of King Christian V, in July 1683 and it was a happy and loving marriage. Anne fell out with her sister, Queen Mary, in 1692 due to Anne's dependence on Sarah Churchill, wife of John Churchill. When Anne became queen, she made Churchill a Knight of the Garter, Master-General of the Ordnance and Captain-General of the army, and appointed Sarah as Mistress of the Robes and Keeper of the Privy Purse. Churchill commanded the Anglo-Dutch forces in the war with France in 1702 and his victories led to Anne making him Duke of Marlborough. He is also known for his crushing defeat of the Franco-Bavarian forces at the Battle of Blenheim during the War of the Spanish Succession in 1704. Political differences finally led to a deterioration of Anne and Sarah's friendship. Anne dismissed Sarah after an argument in 1710 and Marlborough also fell out of favour.

Anne's reign is mainly known for the 1707 Act of Union which united the English and Scottish Parliaments in a parliament of Great Britain which would meet at Westminster. Scotland was to retain its own education, legal and religious systems, but coinage and taxation would be centralised and the union flag (now known as the "old union flag") was created.

Her reign is also known for the divisions over the succession. The 1701 Act of Settlement had settled the succession on Electress Sophia of Hanover and her heirs, but Tories such as Henry St John Viscount Bolingbroke favoured Anne's half-brother James Francis Edward. As Anne lay dying on 30 July 1714 following a stroke, she handed the Lord Treasurer's staff to Charles Talbot, Duke of Shrewsbury, instead of Bolingbroke, thus signalling her support of George of Hanover, son of the late Electress, as her successor. Anne died on 1 August 1714 and was the last monarch of the House of Stuart.

George I

1660-1727

Rule: 1714-1727

Marriages: Sophia Dorothea of Celle, daughter of George William, Duke of Brunswick-Lüneburg.

Issue: 2 children by his wife - George II; Sophia Dorothea of Hanover (married Frederick William I of Prussia). 3 daughters by his mistress Melusine von der Schulenburg.

George I was born on 28 May 1660 at Hanover and was the eldest son of Ernest Augustus, Duke of Brunswick-Lüneburg and Elector of Hanover, and Princess Sophia, Electress of Hanover and granddaughter of James I. Although the childless Queen Anne had many closer relatives, the 1701 Act of Settlement prevented Catholics from inheriting the throne and George was Anne's closest Protestant relation, his mother having died just a few weeks before Anne. He was crowned on 20 October 1714 at Westminster Abbey.

George's marriage to his cousin Sophia Dorothea was not a happy one. George took Melusine von der Schulenburg as a mistress and Sophia Dorothea had an affair with a Swedish count. The count disappeared mysteriously in 1694 and George had his marriage to Sophia Dorothea dissolved. She was imprisoned at the castle at Ahlden in Germany for the rest of her life. The Jacobites spread the rumour that George's eldest son, George Augustus, was not the king's. relationships between the king and Prince of Wales were always strained.

Unfortunately George did not have his mother's gift for languages and had not inherited her love of culture or her lively, engaging manner, so was not a popular king. The Jacobites had been opposed to George becoming king and so tried to depose him and replace him with James Francis Edward Stuart, Anne's half-brother who was Catholic. But they failed.

George I's reign is known for being the beginning of a shift in power from the monarchy to the present day system of a cabinet government led by a prime minister. His frequent absences from Britain meant that he left the governing of the country to a regency council and his cabinet. In 1720, the South Sea Bubble scandal, which saw people becoming destitute overnight and committing suicide, led to George becoming deeply unpopular. He, two of his mistresses and some of his ministers had been involved with the company and were now blamed for the crash. Various members of Parliament were expelled and Robert Walpole rose to power by dealing with the resulting mess. Walpole is seen as Britain's first prime minister, although the title did not exist then, and he led the government from 1721 to 1742.

George I died on 11 June 1727 at Osnabrück in Hanover following a stroke suffered on 9 June. He was buried at Leineschlosskirche, Hanover, but his remains were moved to the mausoleum at Herrenhausen in 1957.

George II

1683-1760

Rule: 1727-1760

Marriages: Caroline of Ansbach (full name: Wilhelmina Charlotte Caroline of Brandenburg-Ansbach), daughter of Margrave John Frederick of Brandenburg-Ansbach.

Issue: 8 children including Frederick, Prince of Wales; Anne (married William IV, Prince of Orange); Amelia; Caroline; William, Duke of Cumberland; Mary (married Frederic II, Landgrave of Hesse-Kassel); Louisa (married Frederick V of Denmark and Norway).

George II is known for being the last British monarch to have been born outside the UK. He was born George Augustus on 10 November (30 October Old Style) 1683 at Herrenhausen Palace, Hanover, and was the only son of George I and his wife Sophia Dorothea of Celle. He was crowned with his wife on 11 October 1727 at Westminster Abbey, with George Frederic Handel writing four anthems for the event.

George's wife Caroline was an intelligent woman and recognised the talents of Robert Walpole, who had risen to be the chief minister in George I's reign. She advised her husband to keep Walpole on and it was he who managed the government on the king's behalf. Walpole's influence in government began to decline in the late 1730s and he resigned after the defeat of the British forces by those of Spain at the Battle of Cartagena de Indias in 1741. He was made Earl of Orford in 1742 and remained one of the king's closest confidantes.

George is also known for being the last British king to fight in battle. In the War of the Austrian Succession, George led the British forces, who were allied with those of Austria, the Netherlands, Hanover and Hesse, to victory against the French at the Battle of Dettingen in 1743.

In 1745, Bonnie Prince Charlie (Charles Edward Stuart, son of the Old Pretender, James Francis Edward Stuart) instigated a Jacobite uprising when he landed in Scotland and began marching south to claim the throne. He defeated the government army at the Battle of Prestonpans, but was defeated at the Battle of Culloden by William Augustus, Duke of Cumberland and son of George II, and his forces. Charles fled abroad into exile.

George II's reign also saw the founding of the British Museum in 1753 (George donated the royal library to the museum in 1757), and the gaining of territory in Canada, Florida and the Caribbean in the Seven Years' War. George died on 25 October 1760 at Westminster Palace at the age of seventy-six. He was on his close stool (toilet chair) when his heart ruptured as the result of an aortic aneurysm. He was buried at Westminster Abbey on 11 November.

George III

1738-1820

Rule: 1760-1820

Marriages: Charlotte Sophia of Mecklenburg-Strelitz

Issue: 9 sons and 6 daughters including George IV; Frederick, Duke of York and Albany; William IV; Charlotte (married King Frederick of Württemberg); Edward, Duke of Kent and Strathearn (father of Queen Victoria); Augusta Sophia; Elizabeth (married Frederick VI, Landgrave of Hesse-Homburg); Ernest Augustus I of Hanover; Augustus Frederick, Duke of Sussex; Mary, Duchess of Gloucester and Edinburgh; Sophia; Amelia.

George III was born on 4 June 1738 at Norfolk House in London and was the eldest son of Frederick, Prince of Wales, and Princess Augusta of Saxe-Gotha. He was the grandson of George II and succeeded him because Frederick, Prince of Wales, died in 1751. His father had died when he was twelve so he was influenced by his tutor John Stuart, Earl of Bute. It was Bute who recommended he marry Charlotte Sophia of Mecklenburg-Strelitz, which he did in September 1761. The marriage was successful, with the couple having fifteen children and appearing devoted to each other.

His early reign was marred by disagreements over the Seven Years' War. George's ex tutor, the Earl of Bute, became the chief minister in government, replacing the Whigs, and his Treaty of Paris was met with opposition due to the concessions made to Spain and France, including the return of some territories. Bute resigned and the Whigs returned to power.

George's reign is known for the loss of the American colonies as a result of the American Revolutionary War and the 1776 Declaration of Independence. However, Britain was victorious in wars with France. After the French Revolution of 1789, France declared war on Great Britain and threatened to invade. This was knocked on the head by Nelson's victory at the Battle of Trafalgar. Trouble with France lasted until 1815 when Napoleon was defeated by the coalition forces led by the Duke of Wellington. George's reign was also known for the British Agricultural Revolution.

George had a keen interest in politics, but in 1788/9 he suffered some type of mental breakdown and left things to William Pitt the Younger, his prime minister. It was Pitt who was largely responsible for the Act of Union of 1800. This act united Great Britain and Ireland as the United Kingdom of Great Britain. In 1801, 1804 and 1810, George suffered further mental collapses and by 1810 he was also suffering from severe cataracts, deafness and rheumatism. His mental state was exacerbated by the death of Princess Amelia in 1810 and in 1811 a regency act was passed making his son Prince Regent. George spent his final years in seclusion at Windsor Castle and died on 29 January 1820 after falling into a coma at Christmas 1819. He was buried in February 1820 in St George's Chapel, Windsor Castle.

George IV

1762-1830

Rule: 1820-1830

Marriages: Maria Fitzherbert; Caroline of Brunswick.

Issue: Charlotte, by Caroline.

George IV was born George Augustus Frederick on 12 August 1762 at St James's Palace, London. He was the eldest son of George III and his wife Charlotte of Mecklenburg-Strelitz. He was a womaniser who was rumoured to have 7000 lockets, containing hair from women he had slept with, by the time of his death. He also loved food and heavy drinking and became a large man, having a waist of 50 inches in 1824.

He secretly married Maria Fitzherbert, a Catholic, a commoner and a woman six years his senior, in December 1785, but the marriage was not valid due to the Royal Marriages Act of 1772, which required the king's consent for a member of the royal family under the age of twenty-five to marry. The 1701 Act of Settlement also barred George from succeeding to the throne if he married a Catholic. In 1795, George III offered to help his son, who was now debt-ridden, if he married Caroline of Brunswick. Neither of them liked the other when they met, but they married on 8 April 1795. It was not a happy marriage and they separated after the birth of their daughter Charlotte.

George ruled Britain as Prince Regent from 1811, due to his father's mental illness, until his accession as king at the age of fifty-seven in 1820 on his father's death. Even though the couple had separated and each had other lovers, Caroline attempted to return to England as George's queen consort. George's ministers began work on a bill (the Pain and Penalties Bill) to annul the marriage and strip her of her title, but the proceedings came to nothing with the bill being withdrawn straight after being passed. Caroline was forcibly prevented from entering Westminster Abbey at George's coronation on 19 July 1821 and subsequently fell ill, dying on 7 August.

George ruled for just ten years, dying on 26 June 1830 at Windsor. He is known for his extravagant lifestyle; the British Regency fashions of his reign; his collection of art; his patronage of architecture; the building of the Royal Pavilion in Brighton; the rebuilding of Windsor Castle and remodelling of Buckingham Palace; and his founding of the National Gallery and King's College, London.

He was buried in St George's Chapel, Windsor Castle in July 1830. His daughter Charlotte had died in 1817, from post-partum complications, so George was succeeded by his brother, William.

William IV

1765-1837

Rule: 1830-1837

Marriages: Adelaide of Saxe-Meiningen, daughter of George I, Duke of Saxe-Meiningen.

Issue: Adelaide had 5 pregnancies - three stillbirths and two living daughters, Charlotte and Elizabeth, who died in infancy. William had 10 children by his mistress Dorothea Bland before he married Adelaide, including Sophia Sidney Baroness De L'Isle and Dudley; Elizabeth Hay, Countess of Erroll; Lady Augusta Gordon; Lord Augustus Fitzclarence; Amelia Cary Viscountess Falkland.

William IV was born on 21 August 1765 at Buckingham Palace, London, and was the third son of George III and Charlotte of Mecklenburg-Strelitz. He came to the throne at the age of sixty-four on 26 June 1830. His brother George IV had died without issue, due to the death of his daughter Charlotte in 1817, and Frederick, Duke of York, the next in line had died in 1827. William is known for being the oldest person to succeed to the British throne.

William was known as the "Sailor King" because he had joined the navy at the age of thirteen and had risen to be Lord High Admiral in 1827. He was good friends with Nelson. He was created Duke of Clarence in 1789 after threatening to stand as a member of the House of Commons if his father didn't grant him a dukedom like his brothers. In 1791, William set up home with Dorothea Bland, stage name Mrs Jordan, and the couple lived together for twenty years and had ten children together. The affair ended when William realised he needed to make a marriage to clear his debts, and Dorothea died in poverty in France in 1816. It took William a few years to make a suitable match, but he married twenty-five-year-old Princess Adelaide of Saxe-Meiningen in July 1818.

William's reign is known for the updating of the Poor Law; the restriction of child labour (1833 Factory Act); the abolition of slavery in most of the British Empire; and the 1832 Great Reform Act, which reformed the electoral system.

William died on 20 June 1837 at Windsor Castle and was buried in the castle's St George's Chapel. He had been determined to live until his niece Victoria, who was next in line, had reached her majority so that her mother, the Duchess of Kent, who the king loathed, would not become regent. Victoria turned eighteen, reaching her majority, on 24 May 1837, so a regency was not required.

Victoria

1819-1901

Rule: 1837-1901

Marriages: Prince Albert of Saxe-Coburg Gotha.

Issue: 9 children: Victoria (m. Frederick III of Prussia); Albert Edward (the future Edward VII); Alice (m. Louis IV, Grand Duke of Hesse); Alfred (m. Grand Duchess Maria Alexandrovna of Russia); Helena (m. Christian of Sonderburg-Augustenburg); Louise (married John Douglas Sutherland Campbell, 9th Duke of Argyll); Arthur (m. Princess Louise Margaret of Prussia); Leopald (m. Princess Helena of Waldeck and Pyrmont); Beatrice (m. Prince Henry of Battenberg).

Queen Victoria was born Alexandrina Victoria on 24 May 1819 at Kensington Palace and was the the only child of Prince Edward Augustus, Duke of Kent and the fourth son of George III, and Princess Victoria Mary Louisa of Saxe-Coburg-Saalfeld, Duchess of Kent. She was known as "Drina" by her family.

Her father died when she was eight months old and she was brought up at Kensington Palace by her mother who, along with her comptroller Sir John Conroy, devised a rigid system of upbringing known as the Kensington System to control Victoria and isolate her from the outside world. When Victoria became queen in 1837, her mother and Conroy expected her to be completely dependent on them, but she rebelled against them and took control of her own life. She was crowned queen at Westminster Abbey on 28 June 1838. Salic law prevented her ruling Hanover and so the crown passed to her uncle who became King Ernest Augustus I.

During the first few years of her reign, she was influenced by Lord Melbourne, the Whig prime minister. His influence ended on her marriage to her cousin, Albert of Saxe-Coburg Gotha, on 10 February 1840. The couple's first child Victoria was born in November 1840 and Victoria went on to have eight more children. Victoria was devastated when Prince Albert died of typhoid fever in December 1861 and wore black for the rest of her life. She also withdrew from public life, preferring to spend her time at Balmoral, Osborne House or Windsor Castle, away from the public eye.

Victoria was the last monarch of the House of Hanover. She is known for being the longest reigning British monarch and the longest reigning female monarch in history.

Victoria's reign is known for the incredible change and progress of the Victorian era; the expansion of the British Empire – making Britain the most powerful country in the world; Victoria being the first Empress of India of the British Raj; the various attempts on the Queen's life; the rumours of an affair with her personal servant John Brown, which caused her to be known as "Mrs Brown"; her Golden Jubilee and the Jubilee Plot (a failed assassination attempt by Irish Nationalists); and the way that she married off her children and grandchildren to European royals, giving her the name "the Grandmother of Europe".

Queen Victoria died on 22 January 1901 at Osborne House, the Isle of Wight. She was eighty-one years old. She was buried in the royal mausoleum at Frogmore House, in Windsor Great Park, beside Prince Albert.

Edward VII

1841-1910

Rule: 1901-1910

Marriages: Alexandra of Denmark, daughter of Christian IX of Denmark.

Issue: 6 children: Albert Victor (died at the age of twenty-eight),
George V (married Princess Mary of Teck);
Louise (married Alexander Duff, Duke of Fife); Victoria;
Maud (married Haakon VII of Norway);
Alexander John, who died the day after his birth.

Edward VII was born on 9 November 1841 at Buckingham Palace and was the eldest son of Queen Victoria and Prince Albert. He was christened Albert Edward and known as Bertie at home. He had a difficult relationship with his father and his mother blamed him for his father's death after Prince Albert died shortly after visiting Edward at Cambridge University in an attempt to get his student son to change his playboy ways. Edward enjoyed gambling, drink and women.

Edward married Princess Alexandra of Denmark in March 1863 and the two went on to have five children who survived into adulthood. Edward was known for his extramarital activities, which led to him being nicknamed "Edward the Caresser", and he was even cited in divorce cases. Women linked to him include actresses Lillie Langtry and Sarah Bernhardt, Lady Randolph Churchill, the Countess of Warwick, and Alice Keppel, great-grandmother of Camilla Parker Bowles.

Edward inherited the throne from his mother Queen Victoria on her death on 22 January 1901 and became Edward VII, King of the United Kingdom, Emperor of India and King of the British Dominions. He was the first British monarch of the House of Saxe-Coburg-Gothe, his father Prince Albert's house, and was the only monarch of this house because his son George V changed the name to the House of Windsor. He reigned for only nine years but was heir apparent for fifty-nine years, two months and thirteen days, his record only being broken by his great-great-grandson Charles, Prince of Wales, in 2011.

His reign was known as the Edwardian period and is known for the progress made in society and technology, and his support of military and naval reforms. He was known as the "Uncle of Europe", being related to most European monarchs, and developed good relations with France.

His last years saw him suffering bouts of bronchitis, no doubt caused by his heavy smoking, and he died on 6 May 1910. He was buried in St George's Chapel, Windsor Castle.

George V

1865-1936

Rule: 1910-1936

Marriages: Mary of Teck.

Issue: 6 children: Edward VIII (later Duke of Windsor); George VI;
Mary (married Henry Lascelles, 6th Earl of Harewood);
Henry, Duke of Gloucester (married Lady Alice Montagu Douglas Scott);
George, Duke of Kent (married Princess Marina of Greece and Denmark);
Prince John.

George V was born on 3 June 1865 at Marlborough House, London, and was the second son of Edward VII and Alexandra of Denmark. He had a naval career from 1877 to 1891 and became the heir apparent when his brother Prince Albert Victor died of influenza in 1892. George inherited the throne on his father's death on 6 May 1910 and held the titles of King of the United Kingdom, Emperor of India and King of the British Dominions. He was the first monarch of the House of Windsor, changing the name of his royal house from Saxe-Coburg-Gothe to Windsor during World War I. He also relinquished all German titles when the war started.

George V was a conventional character, unlike his rather flamboyant playboy father, and enjoyed stamp collecting. He had to give up his love for his cousin Princess Marie of Edinburgh, due to opposition from their mothers, and married Mary of Teck, who had previously been engaged to his older brother, in 1893. The couple became devoted to each other.

His reign is known for the Statute of Westminster, which prepared the way for the creation of the Commonwealth by separating the dominions into separate kingdoms; his visit to India in 1911 (the only king-emperor to visit the country); the outbreak of Word War I; the first Labour government in the UK; the first royal Christmas broadcast (1932); and the rise of Irish Republicanism, communism and fascism.

George V died on 20 January 1936 at Sandringham House, Norfolk, after suffering a catalogue of illnesses including emphysema, pleurisy and bronchitis, due to his heavy smoking. He was buried in St George's Chapel, Windsor Castle.

Edward VIII

1894-1972

Rule: 20 January 1936 – 11 December 1936

Marriages: Wallis Simpson.

Issue: None

Edward VIII was born on 23 June 1894 at White Lodge, Richmond Park, and was the eldest son of George V and Mary of Teck. He was known as "David" to his family. Edward was created Prince of Wales on his sixteenth birthday following his father's accession to the throne. During the First World War he served in the army but Lord Kitchener refused to allow him to fight on the front line.

In the late 1920s, Edward had a series of relationships with married women. He met the twice-married America socialite Wallis Simpson in 1930 and fell head-over-heels in love with her. He was involved with the still-married Wallis when his father George V died on 20 January 1936, making him king. Edward VIII was King of the United Kingdom and British Dominions, and Emperor of India, for less than a year – from 20 January 1936 until 11 December 1936 – making him one of the shortest reigning monarchs in the history of Britain and the Commonwealth. He didn't even get chance to be crowned king.

His reign was cut short not by his death but by his love for Wallis. Edward's prime ministers (both at home and in the Dominions) opposed his plans to marry Wallis, the Church of England being opposed to remarriage after a divorce and the monarch being head of the Church of England. Rather than cause Prime Minister Stanley Baldwin to resign over it and force a general election, Edward decided to abdicate so that he could marry Wallis.

He announced his abdication by radio broadcast on 11 December 1936 and married Wallis on 3 June 1937 in France, following her divorce, After his abdication, Edward became Prince Edward and was made Duke of Windsor on the 8 March 1937. Wallis was never given the title "royal highness", but was known as the Duchess of Windsor. Edward died on 28 May 1972 at his home in Paris and was buried at Frogmore, near Windsor Castle. His wife was laid to rest alongside him when she died in 1986.

George VI

1895-1952

Rule: 1936-1952

Marriages: Lady Elizabeth Bowes-Lyon.

Issue: Elizabeth II; Margaret, Countess of Snowdon

George VI was born Albert Frederick Arthur George on 14 December 1895 at Sandringham House, Norfolk, and was the second son of George V and Mary of Teck. He was named after his great-grandfather Prince Albert, having been born on the anniversary of his death, and was known as "Bertie" by his family. He married Lady Elizabeth Bowes-Lyon, daughter of Claude Bowes-Lyon, Lord Glamis (later 14th Earl of Strathmore and Kinghorne), in 1923 and the couple had two daughters. Before he became king, he served in the Royal Navy and was mentioned in dispatches for his part in the Battle of Jutland in 1916 in World War I.

George became King of the United Kingdom and the Dominions on 11 December 1936 after the abdication of his older brother Edward VIII. He was the first Head of the Commonwealth, the last King of Ireland and the last Emperor of India. His reign is known for the External Relations Act, which was passed by the Irish Parliament to remove the UK monarch from power in Ireland; World War II; and the decline of the power of the British Empire as that of the US and Soviet Union grew.

George was known for his shyness and his stammer, for which he was treated by Lionel Logue, an Australian speech and language therapist. He also suffered from chronic gastric problems.

By the late 1940s, George's health was deteriorating due to the stress of war and lung cancer caused by heavy smoking, so Princess Elizabeth began to take on more royal duties. He had his left lung removed in September 1951 to stop the cancer spreading, but died in his sleep on 6 February 1952 at Sandringham House in Norfolk. He was just fifty-six years old. He was buried in St George's Chapel, Windsor Castle, where he was joined in 2002 by his wife, Queen Elizabeth the Queen Mother. The ashes of his daughter Princess Margaret were also interred in the chapel after her death in 2002.

Elizabeth II

1926-Present

Rule: 1952 - Present

Marriages: Prince Philip of Greece and Denmark.

Issue: Charles, Prince of Wales (married Lady Diana Spencer and divorced in 1996, married Camilla Parker Bowles in 2005); Anne, Princess Royal (married Mark Phillips and divorced him in 1992, married Timothy Laurence in 1992); Andrew, Duke of York (married Sarah Ferguson and divorced in 1996); Edward, Earl of Wessex (married Sophie Rhys-Jones).

Elizabeth II was born Elizabeth Alexandra Mary on 21 April 1926 at 17 Bruton Street, Mayfair, the home of her maternal grandfather Claude Bowes-Lyon, 14th Earl of Strathmore and Kinghorne. She was known to her family as "Lilibet". Elizabeth and her sister Margaret were educated at home by governesses including Marion Crawford, known as "Crawfie". She married Prince Philip of Greece and Denmark, son of Prince Andrew of Greece and Denmark and Princess Alice of Battenberg, in November 1947 after he had renounced his Greek and Danish royal titles, taken on the surname Mountbatten and converted from Greek Orthodoxy to Anglicanism. The couple had been corresponding since Elizabeth was thirteen. They went on to have four children.

Elizabeth became Queen of the United Kingdom and the Commonwealth Realms on 6 February 1952, after the death of her father George VI. She is still the reigning monarch and her other titles include Paramount Chief of Fiji, Duke of Normandy, Lord of Mann and Supreme Governor of the Church of England.

Elizabeth II celebrated her Diamond Jubilee in 2012, marking her sixtieth year as queen. She is the longest living monarch (Queen Victoria is in second place, having lived to eighty-one years and 243 days) and broke Queen Victoria's record of longest reigning monarch (sixty-three years and 216 days) in September 2015. Her eldest son Charles is the longest-serving heir apparent in British history.

Elizabeth II's reign has seen the continuation of the dissolution of the British Empire and the subsequent formation of the Commonwealth of Nations.

Illustrations

Edward the Elder - *The new, impartial and complete history of England from the very earliest period of authentic information, and most genuine records of historical evidence, to the end of the present year.* By Edward Barnard. Published 1790 by Printed for A. Hogg in London
http://tinyurl.com/nr8tb6z

Athelstan - *Will's Cigarette cards,* 1902

Eadred, Aethelred, Edmund Ironside - 'Portraits from Ancient Coins; Edmund I.; Edred; Edwy; Edgar; Edward the Martyr; Ethelred II; Edmund Ironside, 1853, Provenance: *The History of England* by Thomas Gaspey, Esq., Printed & Published by J & F Tallis; London, Edinburgh & Dublin

Edmund II Coat of Arms - Attributed royal Shield of Arms of King Edward the Confessor by Matthew Paris, based on a design on Edward's coins.

Edward the Confessor - Drawn & engraved by James Smith from the Alter Window of Rumford Church. Portrait is from *History of England* London, printed by James Mechell in Fleet Street. 1744

George V - *CanStockPhoto.com* - George V of the United Kingdom (1865-1936) on engraving from the 1800s. King of the United Kingdom and the British Dominions and Emperor of India during 1910-1936.
Engraved by J.S.Virtue & Co.

Edward VII - *istockphoto.com* - "Edward VII (1841-1910) on engraving from 1844. King of the United Kingdom of Great Britain and Ireland and of the British Dominions and Emperor of India during 1901- 1910.
Engraved by G.Cook and published in London by Virtue & Co."

Sweyn Forkbeard Coin - Peter Christian Hauberg (1844-1928) - Hauberg, P. (1900). Myntforhold og Udmyntninger i Danmark indtil 1146.

Edward VIII, George VI & Elizabeth II - Mohammad Rusdianto, Images © MadeGlobal Publishing

ALL OTHER IMAGES - *Cassell's Illustrated History of England, New and Revised Edition (10 Volumes)*, Casell & Company Ltd.

Bibliography

Anglo-Saxons.net - http://www.anglo-saxons.net/

BBC.co.uk - http://www.bbc.co.uk/history/british/

Britannia.com - http://www.britannia.com/

British History Online - http://www.british-history.ac.uk/

Brit Royals - http://www.britroyals.com/

Cassell, John. Cassell's Illustrated History of England (10 volumes), New and Revised Edition. Cassell & Company, Ltd. (1906, first published 1856)

Cavendish, Richard. Kings & Queens: The Concise Guide. David & Charles Ltd, 2007.

Cawthorne, Nigel. Kings & Queens of England. Arcturus Publishing Ltd, 2009.

Crofton, Ian. The Kings and Queens of England. Quercus, 2006.

De Lisle, Leanda. Tudor: The Family Story. Vintage, 2014.Loades, David. The Kings and Queens of England: The Biography. Amberley Publishing, 2013.

Early British Kingdoms - http://www.earlybritishkingdoms.com/

Edward II - http://edwardthesecond.blogspot.com

English Monarchs - http://www.englishmonarchs.co.uk/vikings.htm

Loades, David. Mary Tudor. Amberley Publishing, 2011

The Official Website of the British Monarchy - http://www.royal.gov.uk/

The Anne Boleyn Files - http://www.theanneboleynfiles.com

Tudor History.org - http://tudorhistory.org/

Further Reading

Ackroyd, Peter. Civil War: The History of England Volume III. Macmillan, 2014.

Baldwin, David. Richard III. Amberley Publishing, 2013.

Bartlett, Robert. England under the Norman and Angevin Kings: 1075-1225. OUP Oxford, 2002.

Black, Jeremy. George I (The Yale Monarch Series). Yale University Press UK, 2001.

Black, Jeremy. George III: America's Last King (The Yale Monarch Series). Yale University Press, 2006.

Cannadine, David. George V: The Unexpected King. Allen Lane, 2014.

De Lisle, Leanda. After Elizabeth: The Rise of James of Scotland and the Struggle for the Throne of England. Ballantine Books, 2006.

De Lisle, Leanda. Tudor: The Family Story. Vintage, 2014.

Fraser, Antonia. King Charles II. Phoenix, 2002.

Hibbert, Christopher. Edward VII: The Last Victorian King. Palgrave Macmillan, 2007.

Hibbert, Christopher. Queen Victoria: A Personal History. HarperCollins, 2001.

Ives, Eric. Lady Jane Grey: A Tudor Mystery. Wiley-Blackwell, 2011.

Jones, Dan. The Hollow Crown: The Wars of the Roses and the Rise of the Tudors. Faber and Faber, 2014.

Jones, Dan. The Plantagenets: The Kings Who Made England. William Collins, 2013.

Loades, David. Henry VIII. Amberley Publishing, 2013.

Marr, Andrew. The Diamond Queen: Elizabeth II and Her People. Pan, 2012.

Mortimer, Ian. The Perfect King: The Life of Edward III, Father of the English Nation. Vintage, 2008.

Oliver, Neil. Vikings: A History. Phoenix, 2013.

Penn, Thomas. Winter King: The Dawn of Tudor England. Penguin, 2012.

Porter, Linda. Mary Tudor: The First Queen. Piatkus, 2009.

Russell, Gareth. A History of the English Monarch: From Boadicea to Elizabeth I. MadeGlobal Publishing, 2015.

Schama, Simon. A History of Britain - Volume 1: At the Edge of the World? 3000 BC-AD 1603. Bodley Head, 2009.

Schama, Simon. A History of Britain - Volume 2: The British Wars 1603-1776. Bodley Head, 2009.

Schama, Simon. A History of Britain – Volume 3: The Fate of Empire 1776-2000: Fate of Empire; 1776-2001. BBC Books, 2002.

Skidmore, Chris. Edward VI: The Lost King. Phoenix, 2008.

Smith, E. A. George IV (Yale English Monarch Series). Yale University Press, 1999.

Somerset, Anne. Queen Anne: The Politics of Passion. HarperPress, 2012.

Somerset, Anne. The Life and Times of William IV. Weidenfeld Nicolson Illustrated, 1993.

Starkey, David. Crown and Country: A History of England through the Monarchy. HarperPress, 2011.

Thompson, Andrew C. George II: King and Elector (The Yale Monarch Series). Yale University Press, 2011.

Van der Kiste, John. William and Mary: Heroes of the Glorious Revolution. The History Press, 2008.

Warner, Kathryn. Edward II: The Unconventional King. Amberley Publishing, 2014.

Weir, Alison. Elizabeth the Queen. Vintage, 2009.

Wilson, Derek. The Plantagents: The Kings Who Made Britain. Quercus, 2014.

Ziegler, Philip. George VI: The Dutiful King. Allen Lane, 2014.

Ziegler, Philip. King Edward VIII. HarperCollins, 1990.